Philip Johnson
The Glass House

Philip Johnson

The Glass House

Edited by David Whitney and Jeffrey Kipnis

**Pantheon Books
New York**

Library of Congress Cataloging-in-Publication Data
Philip Johnson : The Glass House / edited by David Whitney
  and Jeffrey Kipnis.
      p. cm.
    ISBN 0-679-42373-7
    1. Glass House (New Canaan, Conn.)   2. Johnson, Philip,
1906– —Criticism and interpretation.   3. Johnson, Philip,
1906– —Homes and haunts—Connecticut—New Canaan.
4. International style (Architecture)—Connecticut—New
Canaan.   5. New Canaan (Conn.)—Buildings, structures,
etc. I. Whitney, David.   II. Kipnis, Jeffrey.
  NA7238.N36P45   1993
  720' .92—dc20   93–18741

Manufactured in the United States of America
First Edition
9 8 7 6 5 4 3 2 1

Contents

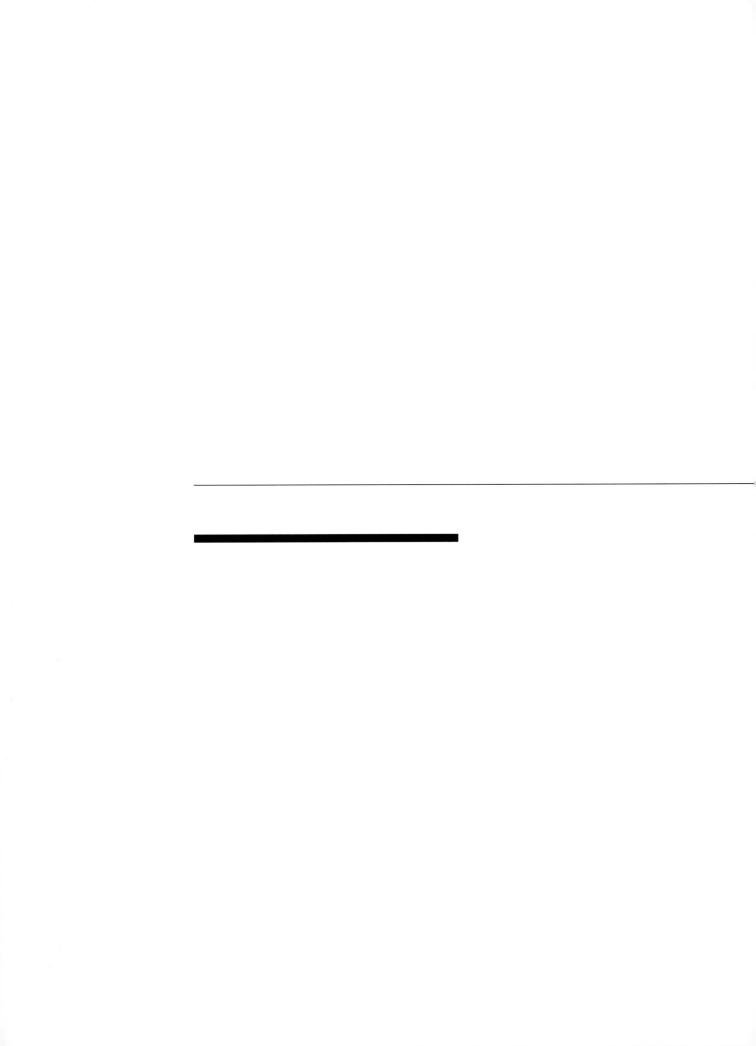

Preface

My place in New Canaan is a kind of "diary of an eccentric architect." I have kept this diary for almost fifty years starting with the purchase of the land in 1946. When I first walked over the original five-acre section (the property today is around forty acres) I sited The Glass House where it is today. The contortions I went through before I actually built the house in 1949 are recorded elsewhere, but the setting on the hill I picked in the first five minutes.

For the last forty years I have gradually, in bits and pieces, made a landscape punctuated by little buildings grouped casually in mown fields marked by farmers' stone walls and decorated by trees in rows, in clumps, in leafy copses conveniently watered by a brook and a pond. How much of this landscaping is the fortuitous use of the existing fields and forests and how much is inspired by my love of English eighteenth-century landscape gardening, I have no idea.

Since 1950 the diary continues with the sometimes chameleonlike quickness of my changes of approach to the art of architecture. The first revolt from "modern" was the 1953 intervention in the Guest House of a double-domed skeleton of a room within a room. The aim of the design was to arrange the light sources from outside the "room" as in the breakfast room in Sir John Soane's house in London.

That change did not affect the landscape. More radical was the Pavilion—the folly—"floating" in a pond I excavated in the valley below the house in 1962. The design is a false scale pavilion (you might hit your head in the arches) made up of 8-foot squares arranged more or less like a

Mondrian. I derived the "toe-ing" of the columns from Delaunay's famous painting of the Gothic church of St. Severin. He spread the lower part of the columns, a motif that I utilized in later buildings in Nebraska and New York. My main concern, however, was to create a corner column that would keep the module without the Renaissance problem of "disappearing" columns in the interior corners of the arcades.

The third addition is the Painting Gallery, added in 1965, on land north of the original five acres. Since I did not intend to add new buildings too close to The Glass House, I made a berm around it. The cloverleaf shape of the gallery was a result of the functional solution: a central column in each "leaf" carrying a screen for pictures, like a Rolodex or a postcard rack. Different-sized circles provided three differently scaled picture-hanging "walls." The entrance to the almost underground "Kunstbunker," as it was called by critics, is similar to the "Tomb of Atreus" in the Peloponnesus, Greece: solemn and important.

Down the path from the Painting Gallery came the Sculpture Gallery of 1970. Even farther from The Glass House, its white painted brick stands out in the bucolic surroundings. This time I played with interlocking volumes, the roof being 45 degrees offset from the floor. The gabled roof is diagonal to the floor layout. This building is "modern," perhaps, but there is the idea of the plan—a central court with four

bays opening out—which is surely classical. The floors of these bays are on five different levels, however, depending on the type of sculpture to be displayed.

Then comes the later addition to the south, a white stucco studio of 1980. A monk's cell by intent, it has a vaguely Islamic look due to a domelike truncated cone over the worktable and a minaretlike chimney in one corner. A single small window allows one to observe the weather and Nature (Frank Lloyd Wright always capitalized Nature).

In 1984 I built below the Studio a 15-foot by 15-foot construction of galvanized chain-link fencing in honor of my friend Frank Gehry, who favors using this material. Lilies grow inside, while the omnivorous deer are kept out. The building is architecturally a fantasy, symmetrical with a 45-degree pitched gable, as a child would sketch a house. It sits romantically on a nineteenth-century footing of a cow barn now long gone (the pleasures of ruins!).

In 1985 I designed a tower dedicated to Lincoln Kirstein. Placed in the landscape to make a point of interest, it punctuates the panorama from the house. The tower is in actuality a very steep and precarious stairway.

In all my recent work I strive for nostalgia, precariousness, sexual yearning. I am not sure whether or not Freud could have fun with these peculiar impulses, but I always hope some of these feelings can be transferred to stone and steel.

In the lake pavilion, for example, the

small scale gives the visitor a feeling of all-importance, superiority over the environment. The fact that the Pavilion is an island gives a romantic feeling of impregnable solitariness. My footbridge to the art galleries is quite scary: too narrow and springy. You might fall off? The Glass House: the glass might shatter in the wind! In the Lincoln Kirstein Tower there are no railings on the stairs. Again, you might fall off! All these feelings must be, of course, faint. A truly dangerous situation would be counter-attractive and counter-architectural.

The tower is built of concrete block, a not beautiful but cheap and, for my purposes, perfect material since I needed a small module that could give scale and make my staircase precarious.

As I write in the winter of 1993, on the drafting board is what may be the last building on my property. I am planning a small parking lot with an attendant tower building to create a Visitors' Center when the owner of the property, the National Trust for Historic Preservation, takes over. The design was begun a year after my Deconstructivist Exhibit of 1988 at The Museum of Modern Art. I was much influenced by the work of these young (to me) men and women. The result is the present design, my appreciation of some of influences of these "kids," as I have been calling them.

The diary is probably complete. There are some new ideas floating in the peculiar recesses of my mind but there may not be the opportunity to build them here.

Anyhow, I do not need any new architecture here. I like it the way it is.

Philip Johnson 2/3/93

Jeffrey Kipnis

Introduction: Throwing Stones—
The Incidental Effects of a Glass House

Whatever other debates it may engender, one fact is indisputable. No other episode in the history of twentieth-century architecture can compare with the one staged in New Canaan, Connecticut, by Philip Johnson, America's most renowned and controversial architect. For over forty years, Johnson's Glass House and the additions he has made to its surrounds have continuously demanded the attention of scholars, critics, and the popular press alike, making it one of the most widely publicized works of modern architecture in the world.

However the Johnson estate is understood—as a collection of buildings, pavilions, and follies assembled by Philip Johnson the Curator, as a working sketchbook drawn by Philip Johnson the Architect, as an evolving microcosm designed by Philip Johnson the Landscape Architect, as a diary reflecting upon developments in architecture written by Philip Johnson the Critic-Historian, or as a publicity event of remarkable longevity choreographed by Philip Johnson the Media Star—one cannot deny the sway this elusive enterprise has held and continues to hold.

Each of these characterizations belongs to a different critical perspective; indeed, over the years The Glass House has become a signpost for the vicissitudes of architectural thought.[1] As new ideas have arisen, critics have often used the occasion of a reconsideration of the Johnson estate to elaborate their consequences. Thus, critics have not visited The Glass House as much as they have revisited it.

The urge to return again and again to New Canaan has been fueled, in part, by

Johnson's periodic additions to the original design, such as the pond, the Pavilion, the Galleries, the Study, and so on. As one surveys the history of these, one cannot help but sense an exquisite timing in their execution and a provocateur's hand in their design. It is as if, aside from whatever other role each addition was to perform, it was always also intended to spark new interest. Whether cultivated intentionally or not, the effect has been dramatic; over four decades, almost every mention of Johnson in the press makes reference to The Glass House.

Like a restless child bored with his toys, Johnson incessantly sought justifications for adding elements to the complex, often experimenting with a stylistic innovation that caught his eye at the time. In the periods between these additions, he fiddled compulsively with the details of landscape, cutting trees, installing and removing works of art, and so on. This process continues today; at the time of this writing, the architect is in the midst of designing at least two more projects for the site.

Each new construction fundamentally transformed the context and reset the character of the previously existing buildings, rendering prior interpretations vulnerable and opening the door to critical reassessment. To make matters more complicated, Johnson frequently endorsed the new interpretive perspective, incorporating its themes into his own ongoing account. Virtually from its inception, The Glass House, the architect, and its many interpreters have woven an unending and intricate conversational network that resembles nothing so much as a spider's web. Thus, perhaps more than any other architectural masterpiece preceding it, The Glass House is in a process of evolution inseparable from its evolving commentary. No experience of it, no retelling of its story, no rethinking of its content nor reestimation of its merits can disentangle itself from this web.

Throughout his career, the otherwise mercurial Philip Johnson has remained steadfastly faithful to one principle alone: that architecture is first, foremost, and finally a visual art. In Johnson, architecture-as-art has found a formidable champion. When some argued that in architecture, art must always serve function, Johnson placed function in the service of art; when others argued that architecture was more a matter of history than art, Johnson made art out of history. The ancient dispute of priorities between form as the source of beauty and form as the bearer of meaning has animated the development of The Glass House, setting the stage for some of the most vigorously contested debates in architecture to occur during the past two decades.

In fact, the first and most influential critical revisiting of The Glass House was by Johnson himself in his 1950 *Architectural Review* essay "House at New Canaan,

Connecticut," published almost immediately after construction of the original scheme was completed. In this essay, Johnson sets out a comprehensive account of the various sources for his design. His list mixes such estimable antecedents as Ledoux, Schinkel, Choisy, Malevitch, Le Corbusier, and Mies van der Rohe with such oddities as a reference to Count Pückler's estate at Muskau in Silesia, a stock steel and glass construction detail, and an anecdotal memory of a burnt wooden village.

The importance of this essay both to contemporary architectural design and discourse cannot be overstated. Of course it shaped the scholarly treatment of The Glass House. Beyond that, however, it established The Glass House as a watershed for much of the architecture to follow, for its irreverent recombination of incongruent materials provided a cornerstone strategy for postmodernism. Finally, the essay demonstrated the instrumental value of a tool that would eventually come to be commonplace in the discipline: the critical essay written by the architect about his own project.

Many other architects before Philip Johnson had written on their own work, describing the effects they hoped to achieve or setting out their polemic vision. Like a parenthetical thought, however, these writings always occupied a secondary position vis-à-vis the design, respecting if not valorizing the primacy of the actual building. Johnson's text on The Glass House, on the other hand, quickly assumed a status equal to that of The Glass House itself. Soon one was unthinkable without the other; they became, and remain, inseparable.

Eventually, Johnson would witness the coequivalence between theory and design he achieved with his 1950 essay underwrite a new form of practice—as purveyed by such diverse architect-theorists as Robert Venturi, Leon Krier, and Rem Koolhaas, and then carried to an extreme by Bernard Tschumi and Peter Eisenman. These latter architects systematically attached theoretical texts to their design on the principle that the project itself existed only as the two taken together. Viewing such proposals as an overintellectualization of the art of architecture, Johnson came to disdain the very practice that his own work foreshadowed. In characteristic fashion, however, he supported the design activities of these architects because, as he put it, he liked the sculptural quality of their forms.

Johnson's ambivalence, his equivocation between the intellectual and visual sides of architecture, ever engaging in the former while ever extolling the latter, is a fundamental conflict for the architect that operates throughout his career as a designer. Perhaps for these reasons, he never repeated his critical undertaking at The Glass House. Though he often writes about his subsequent work in New Canaan and elsewhere, citing sources and so on, in these later remarks he always uses a more traditional form of explanation and always emphasizes the aesthetics of the work.

Johnson's own graphic design for "House at New Canaan," as well as his rhetorical style in its capsule descriptions, gave the essay its decisive tone. There is little doubt, moreover, that one can readily find in his original design the presence of the references he cites. But is this essay truly the encyclopedic catalogue of sources it claims to be?

Today, those who know Johnson would be less enthralled by the authoritative demeanor of the essay. These confidants would know well the architect's uncanny ability to put forward a cogent and uncompromising position, only to reverse himself a few minutes later with complete confidence and persuasive force. In his work as well as his personal life, Johnson is always the consummate purveyor of effects. His agile mind suffers none of Emerson's hobgoblins and has little patience for the pedantries of the truth. To Goethe's charge that the pilaster was a lie, Johnson adjusted his tie and replied, "Yes, but what a delightfully useful one."

Yet there are many other reasons to question the limitations of Johnson's original list of sources. As the estate grew and transformed, Johnson amended the list and, on occasion, even suggested a different genealogy. For example, by the time he is discussing his thoughts on the property with the art critic Rosamond Bernier in 1986, his story focuses on his landscaping intentions, ideas only vaguely suggested in

his 1950 essay. Also, there is the evidence of the dozens of developmental sketches leading up to the final design. These sketches, which come to play a central role in discussions of The Glass House in the late seventies, indicate other influences, ones that he does not mention.

But perhaps the most glaring omission was the essay's understatement of the history of the idea of a glass house, whose allure had developed, along different trajectories, for over three hundred years. With conspicuous restraint, Johnson writes that "the idea of The Glass House came from Mies van der Rohe." And no doubt it is true enough that the specific stimulus that launched the architect on his three-year obsession to build a glass house for himself was Mies's 1947 sketch for the Farnsworth House. But hidden within this simple attribution to Mies was a complex and powerful idea.

Philip Johnson knew from the very moment he saw Mies's sketches that there was much more to the issue than the material, tectonic, and formal problem of constructing a house whose walls were entirely of glass. He knew that his Glass House would exercise an extraordinary power over the imagination of professional and layperson alike. More than most, Johnson the architectural curator and historian knew that history almost guaranteed the effect.

He knew of Hardwick Hall, whose façade, "more glass than wall," fascinated English society at the beginning of the seventeenth century. Perhaps the Elizabethan poet and moralist George Herbert already envisioned the long-term implications of Hardwick when he immortalized the trend to transparency two decades after its completion in his aphorism "Whose house is of glass, must not throw stones at another."

Johnson knew the history of the glass-house conservatory, such as the Great Conservatory at Chatsworth built by the gardener Joseph Paxton with Decimus Burton for the sixth Duke of Devonshire, a descendant of Bess of Hardwick. Burton went on to collaborate with Richard Turner in such famed glass houses as the Palm House at Kew Gardens, but when Paxton's Crystal Palace of 1851 stunned the world, the mesmerizing power of glass architecture became evident in full measure.

Johnson knew the fascination that glass held for the German architectural avant-garde of 1910 to 1920. Besides his familiarity with Mies's visionary projects for glass skyscrapers from the period, he would have known of Paul Scheerbart's *Glasarchitektur*, a polemic tract glorifying glass as the material par excellence of modernism. He also would have known of the architectural group *Die Gläserne Kette* (the Glass Chain) and, in particular, of the stir generated by its most renowned member, Bruno Taut, when he built the Glass House in Cologne in 1914.

He knew all this and much more—from the dizzying ecstasy of reflections in the Hall of Mirrors at Versailles to the ephemeral transparency of Gropius's glass walls at the Bauhaus. In short, the architect knew that for over three centuries, the history of architecture was, as Le Corbusier put it, "the history of the struggle for the window," and that his house would rivet attention as it brought that history to its most daring conclusion.

And, as was to become his habit, Johnson was dead right. Before construction was finished, *The New York Times* was already reporting that throngs of uninvited visitors were creating traffic jams on Ponus Ridge as they looked upon his "ultra-modern residence" with "awe, wonder and indignation."

As might be expected, initial popular reaction to the house was preoccupied more with its material vulnerability and its unscreening of private life than with the intricacies of modern design. On the other hand, more learned studies of the work pay little attention to the voyeuristic implications of The Glass House, debating instead the formal, spatial, tectonic, and cultural themes of the work. When the issue of the glass walls arises in these writings, it is in terms of the reflections, vistas, and framed views that these afford the occupant. This is, of course, as it should be, for however delighted the architect may have been with the popular effect of the house, he struggled over the design for three years in order to produce a rigorous work of architectural art, one that would substantially rethink the problem of modernism.

Yet at least one bit of evidence suggests that the exhibitionist motif of the house was never far from the mind of this master of the architectural exhibition. In his 1950 essay, the image that Johnson chose to introduce The Glass House was the remarkable Arnold Newman photograph (see page 13), which captures the building's richest visual effects, from its panoramic views to the vertiginous collage of its multiple reflections. But what gives this photograph its edge, what makes it so unnerving even today, is that it casts the viewer as a Peeping Tom. With more than a hint of prurient pleasure, we steal a glance across the bedroom to catch Johnson sitting at his desk with his back to us, reading. We know he is unaware of our staring at him—that is, unless he happens to catch our furtive reflection in the pane of glass he faces.

Though each of the other elements of the original scheme was eventually revised—the interior of the Brick Guest House was redesigned, the Lipschitz sculpture was sold, and the driveway was relocated—The Glass House itself remains today exactly as it was upon completion in 1950 in every detail except two. The Johnson candelabra and the Giacometti sculpture, *Night*, both of which figure prominently in early photographs of the interior, are absent. Not much more is to be made of the disappearance of the odd, medieval candelabra than simply to point out that Johnson's considerable talent for architecture and interior design has never extended to the design of furnishings. Within weeks after finishing

the interior, the architect removed the clumsy fixture.

The disappearance of the Giacometti, however, was entirely accidental. The sculpture began to shed plaster and was returned to the artist to be repaired. Giacometti stripped off all of the plaster down to the wire frame, but died before he had a chance to reconstitute the work. The sculpture was lost and not replaced; nevertheless, its situation in the original interior is worth further consideration.

The genius of The Glass House obtains from the fact that, although it derives its style from modernism, the discrete, ordered space it engenders belongs more to classical architecture. There is little disagreement among critics on this point, though the argument persists as to whether this is a contribution to or a detraction from the development of modern architecture. The quarrel is most frequently staged in terms of a comparison between The Glass House and Mies van der Rohe's Farnsworth House. Though the Farnsworth House is the immediate predecessor of The Glass House, Mies's design is directed toward the exact opposite effect. In the Farnsworth House, Mies redeploys all of the components of a neoclassical house in order to achieve the characteristic flowing, continuous space of canonic modern architecture.

Every detail, every nuance of Johnson's design operates to merge the modern into the classical, and in his interior the architect brings the effect to a climax. Within the confines of an 1,800-square-foot box, Johnson uses the Miesian furniture, the modern fixtures and cabinets, the works of art, and the fireplace to zone the open space into an intricate organization containing as much differentiation and hierarchy as a Georgian mansion, complete with wainscoted walls. In order to accomplish this extraordinary condensation of the modern and the classical, the architect multiplies the tasks performed by each interior element.

Thus, for example, the Poussin painting serves as a work of art, as a wall delimiting the room within which the living room sits, as a door to the bedroom, as an object floating in the intermediate register of the section, layering the space into three floors, and as an edge of the modeled residual space outlined in remainder by the fireplace, the closet wall, and the edge of the carpet. The significance of this leftover space and the others like it punctuating the scheme should not be discounted, for nooks and other residual spaces are signatures of the classical plan while anathema to the modern plan. And, as Venturi observed in *Complexity and Contradiction*, often the most interesting spaces in architecture are residual.

Since Johnson has never shown the slightest hesitation to revise his work in New Canaan, we must conclude that he has left the interior of The Glass House unchanged because to his eye and mind it is perfect. Yet in this context of precise and meticulous overdetermination, what are we to make of the accidental disappearance of the Giacometti? Did fate wrest a pivotal detail from the space?

Alberto Giacometti's eerily elongated figures have stimulated endless interpretations; many have seen them as meditations upon the existential isolation of modern man, for example. But for an architect, the most enviable quality of these sculptures is their uncanny ability to articulate a vast, almost infinite, space, the very space that Mies, Le Corbusier, and others sought for modern architecture. Thus, to find a Giacometti as a centerpiece in the most explicitly bound area of The Glass House, poised precariously at the edge of the coffee table so as to emphasize the limitlessness of the space it commands, is to encounter a stunning spatial counterpoint. It is as though the purpose of the sculpture was to render the finite, domestic space of the living room once again infinite, to merge, that is, the modern and the classical.

The duality of the modern and the classical contained within The Glass House may account, in part, for the cool reception received by its counterpart in the original scheme, the Brick Guest House. Most critics gloss over the original design of the Brick House, focusing instead on its role in the site. But Arthur Drexler, whose 1949 review was the only major treatment of The Glass House to be published before Johnson's *Architectural Review* essay took control of the discourse, is brutal in his dismissal of it. In an essay marked by brilliant insights as well as stunning boners, Drexler sums up the virtue of the Brick Guest House with rapier in cheek, writing that "under certain circumstances, the attractiveness of a house can be gauged according to its resemblance to a prison." Five years after the publication of this essay, Johnson chose Drexler to succeed him as architectural curator of The Museum of Modern Art.

In fact, the Brick House serves its primary functions in the site design very well: it frames the arrival and fixes one of the vertices of the triangular organization of the three elements of the original scheme: The Glass House, the Brick House, and the sculpture. Finally, with The Glass House, it set up the parallel sheering essential to the dynamics of the site. But the form and materiality of the Brick House suggested a certain equivalency in opposition to The Glass House: two rectangular prisms, one solid, one void. The apparent equivalency created an expectation about the interior of the Brick House that it did not fulfill. If the two were truly equal but opposite, the interior space of the Brick House should have been as complex and textured as that of The Glass House, with contrary themes. Not only did the restricted scale of the Brick House make such an achievement unlikely, but more importantly, The Glass House interior already contained its own spatial oppositions.

Thus it was that in 1952, Johnson undertook his first major revision of the original scheme, converting the interior of the Brick House into his master bedroom. Lifting vaults from the Soane House, Johnson set these within the Brick House, floating in front of walls resurfaced with textured Fortuny fabric.

Finally, he back-lit the arches, creating the romantic illusion of a sunset. When he wrote of the renovation eleven years later, he did not mention the obvious historical reference; instead, he focused on the feeling of the space. "The domes in my guest room . . . have a calming, quieting effect on the guests—most enjoyable." Here, then, another conversion is complete, for now Johnson is strictly the artist of visual experience and no longer the scholar-architect.

With the renovation of the Brick House, the architect began a pattern that would be repeated in many of the additions to come, one that confirmed Drexler's early intuition that the entire complex was best understood as a single house. Again and again, Johnson took one part of the functional program already contained within the original scheme—for example, the painting gallery or the study—split it off, and elaborated it into a new and independent construction on the site. In keeping with that pattern, Johnson worked for several years on the design of a dining pavilion to be located north of The Glass House, before abandoning the idea. Thus, each addition was like a new wing enlarging the complex-as-house. The partitioning of functions into individual forms was, of course, a residue of modernism; hence, as the estate grew larger and moved further from a modernist aesthetic, ironically, it moved closer to its principles of space planning.

After the initial five years of activity, The Glass House slipped into relative quietude. Johnson turned most of his attention elsewhere, to his collaboration with Mies van der Rohe on the Seagram Building and to his own designs for museums in Utica, New York, and Fort Worth, Texas. In New Canaan, he slowly started to acquire additional land, beginning with the parcel to the north of The Glass House, the site of the unrealized dining pavilion.

Initially, Johnson was reluctant to purchase more property and had to be goaded into buying the house that overlooked The Glass House southeast from Ponus Ridge Road. While visiting the architect in 1956, Libby Holman, the actress and torch singer, noticed the house. When she learned that it was occupied, she chided the architect in no uncertain terms for compromising his (and her) privacy in such a way. He bought the property, dividing the house into an apartment for his butler and a summer home for his sister; currently, it is occupied by the caretaker and his family.

But when Johnson finally decided to rouse The Glass House from its eight-year repose, he did it with a splash. In 1962, he completed construction of the pond, complete with a 100-foot jet fountain, as well as the notorious Pavilion, his obscene gesture to the puritanical functionalists dominating architecture at the time. The indignant response to the Pavilion was immediate. Kenneth Frampton wrote: "Although it is passed off by the architect as a 'folly' by virtue of its entirely false scale, it is, nonetheless, in its trivial historicism, quite typical of Johnson's recent work. . . . It is hard to believe that this is the same man who once designed and built the . . . famous Glass House in which he still lives, or that a former admirer and collaborator of Mies can, in a few years, come to conceive such feeble forms as these."

Writing as technical editor, Frampton published his comments in England's *Architectural Design*, without a byline, an omission he would go to some pains to correct nearly two decades later.

Johnson reveled in the attack, responding to Frampton's commentary "that we need more of this pointed, beautifully written criticism in this country!" Undeterred and completely in his element, he went on the warpath in the name of architecture as art. In a series of articles and lectures, he attacked the prevailing tendency toward bland, utilitarian architecture, frequently using the Pavilion as his opening volley. As usual, he laid out the historical references for the design, but a noticeable shift occurred from his earlier, academic, appeal to antecedents. Historical material was borrowed for the sake of its intrinsic beauty, and from that point on, beauty and experiential delight became the hallmarks of Johnson's approach to design and criticism.

In addition to the well-rehearsed features of the Pavilion—its illusionistic, reduced scale and its overt classicism—there are other aspects of its design that are of particular interest to the evolution of The Glass House. Though anticipated by the Brick House renovation, the flippant classical style of the Pavilion seemed jarring to many, as if a noisy alien had landed uninvited upon the serene, modern field established by the original scheme. However, its roots may be found in the developmental sketches for The Glass House itself.

During the course of its design, Johnson experimented with over two dozen distinct versions of The Glass House. Most studied different massing or organizational relationships between The Glass House and Brick Guest House. A few others attempted to unify the two houses into a single scheme, and one of these clearly suggested the pinwheel arrangement of the Pavilion. But the most blatant evidence that the stylistic issues of the Pavilion were on Johnson's mind as early as 1948 is to be found in the so-called Syrian Arch scheme. These sketches, like the Pavilion itself, seem to come out of nowhere and show the architect flirting with the idea of configuring one of the walls of The Glass House as a series of three arches. The enigmatic scheme disappeared almost as quickly as it arrived.

From the perspective of these sketches, the Pavilion appears to be something of a repository for ideas that the architect developed for The Glass House but did not use and yet did not want to discard. John-

son went so far as to treat the Pavilion like an alter ego of The Glass House. As if to supplement its missing rooms, he named the Pavilion's four spaces the entrance hall, the library, the living room, and the boudoir.

The design of the Pavilion shows the architect for the first time explicitly using the estate, as Frampton suggests, to work out ideas for major commissions elsewhere. Also, in both its historical postmodernism and its reflection upon the column designs of Minuro Yamasaki, the Pavilion is a clear commentary on prevailing architectural issues at the time. Thus, it sets into motion two of the interpretations of the Johnson estate which others would develop, and which the architect would adopt: that it is a sketchbook for his own work and a diary of his thoughts on the work of other architects.

Johnson has remained a staunch devotee of the Pavilion since its inception. As late as 1977, in a discussion with Calvin Tomkins, art critic for *The New Yorker*, Johnson devoted more time to the Pavilion than to any other work in New Canaan. Yet the folly has never earned the respect Johnson felt it deserved and did not find an unequivocal admirer in the critical community until 1986, when Vincent Scully revisited The Glass House. Even Robert Stern, the architect's best student at Yale and, later, the most ardent advocate of Johnson's historicist postmodernism, did not find the design quite satisfying. However, for Stern the problem with the Pavilion is not that it is frivolous, but that it is not frivolous enough!

The furor over the Pavilion preempted recognition of the more fundamental mutation of the complex effected by the pond and, to a lesser extent, the fountain. The pond expanded the original scheme from a complex into an estate, and transformed the space of The Glass House from a tightly knit relationship among forms to that of the relationship between the forms and the landscape. From then on, all of Johnson's work in New Canaan was affected by landscaping issues. Though Johnson had been discussing the estate in terms of English landscape design since he completed the pond and Pavilion, it was not until 1970, when *Time* magazine's art critic, Robert Hughes, described The Glass House as belonging to the tradition of eighteenth-century ducal estates, that the issue came to the fore in criticism.

Another change occurred in 1960 that had as profound an effect on the further evolution of The Glass House as any architectural event, for it was then that Philip Johnson met and began a relationship with David Whitney. Whitney's most palpable influence at The Glass House is on the art collection. For years, Johnson purchased art, and his most publicized acquisitions were those advised by the legendary Alfred Barr, founder of The Museum of Modern Art—Johnson's first employer and best friend. But it was David Whitney who molded Johnson into a collector. Under the curator's guidance, Johnson assembled a coherent collection of contemporary American art of astonishing quality, containing important works by such artists as Johns, Warhol, Stella, Heizer, Salle, Schnabel, and Fischl.

The collection Johnson and Whitney assembled ultimately stimulated the architect to add two major buildings to the estate, the Painting Gallery in 1965 and the Sculpture Gallery in 1970. It would be a misrepresentation, however, to restrict Whitney's influence on The Glass House to issues surrounding the art. An avid gardener in his spare time, Whitney advised Johnson on many of his landscaping decisions. As Johnson tells it, "David and I sit outside The Glass House and argue for hours over which trees to cut and which to keep." Of course, such decisions do not appear in any journal; nevertheless, the ineffable refinement of the space of the estate today is a result of their cumulative effect.

Johnson once invited a landscape architect to offer his recommendations for the estate. Over lunch in The Glass House, the expert suggested familiar ideas about paths and terracing. As he was departing, he stepped out of The Glass House, turned to the two and asked, "By the way, where is the main house?" The only remains of that visit is the anecdote. Johnson hired many consultants, but, fortunately, he listened to very few.

The period 1960 to 1973 was a time of enormous energy and activity at The Glass House—architectural, intellectual, and social. During this period, Johnson completed his remaining land acquisitions and made major changes to the estate. He purchased an additional parcel to the north, site of the painting and sculpture galleries, and another to the south, where the new driveway, the study, and the chain-link fence house are located. Finally, Johnson acquired a last parcel still farther south, on which David Whitney's turn-of-the-century, shingle-style house sits. Later, Whitney added to this house a square, granite-walled heather garden designed by the architect. After Johnson decided to donate the estate to the National Trust, his neighbor, Audrey Phipps Holden, gave the Trust an additional eight acres to the far northwest, bringing the total to forty acres.

The final revision of the original scheme occurred in 1964, when Johnson moved the S-curve driveway to its current location. Moving the driveway sacrificed an unintended formal feature of the original design, but better fulfilled the experiential program Johnson initially hoped to achieve. In the first version, as you drove down the driveway, you caught a momentary glimpse of the east façade of the Brick Guest House through an opening in the trees. The virtual axis created by this frontal presentation of the brick wall articulated by three round windows was more akin to Roman than Greek planning. Afterward, you proceeded round a tree quite near the Brick House and then into the car

park, where The Glass House unfolded on the oblique.

In the current version, you proceed down the longer, more picturesque driveway, through trees that screen both Glass House and Brick House until the last moment. Then, as you pass the trees, the curtain rises on the complex, presenting first the Brick House and then, at a distance, and partly screened by a wall, The Glass House. Now both houses are obliquely revealed, in better accord with the principles of Choisy, so admired by Johnson.

Soon after the driveway revision, the architect codified his ideas about arrival and procession in his essay "Whence and Whither: The Processional Element of Architecture." Many architectural theorists consider his reintroduction of processional considerations to modern architecture to be among his most significant contributions. While such ideas may seem appropriate and even commonplace today, they were in fact quite subversive in the intellectual climate of modern planning that still prevailed at the time.

In order to achieve a more neutral, objective space and to shift the political focus of architecture from the individual to the collective, modernist architects rejected planning ideas that took advantage of single viewpoint effects, such as perspective or oblique screening. Not only were such effects illusionistic and dishonest, they reasoned, but they unduly celebrated the individual, particularly the few privileged enough to enjoy them. Thus, for Johnson to subordinate modernism's loftier goals to discredited experiences was nothing less than a heresy to the apostles of modernism's political project. To Johnson, for whom such political arguments were nonsense, it was merely a matter of designing the most pleasurable visual experience. Since 1965, the architect's ideas have gained wide acceptance, though the controversy surrounding them remains unsettled.

The formal and spatial changes of the estate in the sixties were paralleled by transformations in its social life. During the late fifties, social activity at The Glass House consisted primarily of architectural discussions Johnson held for students. Over time, these discussions gave way to luncheons or lawn parties for friends and distinguished guests. The increasing pitch of social activities during the sixties brought a semipublic atmosphere to The Glass House, which came to be embodied in the two institution-like buildings Johnson added to the estate during the period, the Painting Gallery and the Sculpture Gallery.

The Painting Gallery (1965) was announced as a paraphrase of the ancient Treasury of Atreus at Mycenae, but such architectural allusions had by then lost their coin for many critics, who found other aspects of the Gallery more to their liking. The exception to the rule was Vincent Scully, a critic whose greatest joy derives from his unparalleled ability to see something ancient in almost everything. Not content with the relatively recent vintage of the Treasury, purportedly built in the fourteenth century B.C., Scully preferred to detect in the Gallery shades of the earth goddess as drawn in the plans of the neolithic temples of Malta.

In any case, such blatant allusions may have lost some of their luster for Johnson as well. After the Painting Gallery, there would be no more overt quotations of historical precedents in New Canaan. Instead, the subsequent work drew its energies more and more from developments in contemporary architecture.

Of greater interest to writers at the time were the gallery's display system and its siting. Johnson mounted the paintings on screens hung from circular tracks in the ceiling of the round bays that served as storage wells. This system enabled the architect to rehang the gallery space at liberty by rotating desired paintings to the front. Such hanging techniques were well known, but Johnson integrated them into the overall design concept with notable precision. Each circular bay is of a different diameter, accommodating paintings of different sizes, and the radial screens can be aligned to create a rectangular gallery within the orbital plan.

Though it is often described as such, the Painting Gallery, nicknamed the *Kunstbunker*, is not underground. It sits above ground, though covered in sod so as to appear a chthonic mound emerging from the landscape. For Johnson, who loves artifacts, the design of the *Kunstbunker* was a concession to his developing conception of The Glass House as a garden estate. He amplified the impression with two devices borrowed from landscape architecture: a footbridge to take one out of the formalist space of the original complex and into nature, and a moon-viewing platform, which was sited opposite the entry corridor to the gallery.

The hyperkinetic decade at The Glass House came to a climax with the 1970 opening of the spectacular Sculpture Gallery, which may not only be Philip Johnson's best work of architecture in New Canaan, eclipsing even The Glass House itself, but the architect's best non-high-rise building, period. Moreover, the Sculpture Gallery served as a sketch-study for Johnson's pinnacle achievement in high-rise architecture, Pennzoil Place.

Informed but unfettered by direct reference either to historical or contemporary sources, the Gallery is a wholly original work. In this étude of acute angles and sectional circulation, Johnson created a space so vast that it appears unable to be filled, whether occupied by one person or a hundred people. Though not public, neither is the gallery entirely private.

As one descends through the Sculpture Gallery's five levels staged over two floors, one's sense of existential isolation in the space causes each *ad hoc* encounter with the sculpture to be at once intimate and empty. The effect is intensified by a collection that consists largely of pop and minimalism, that is, works exploring anonymity, mass production, and the banal. No collaboration between architecture and art could more thoroughly erase both the humanist and the modernist subject to such dazzling effect. In those terms, Johnson's Sculpture Gallery achieves results that deconstructivist architecture would pursue a decade later—though, unlike the deconstructivists, Johnson achieved his ends through a detailed study of the architectures of humanism and modernism.

The recession of the early seventies brought Johnson's activities in New Canaan—social and architectural—almost to a halt. The estate entered into a second dormancy; when at the end of the decade it became active again, it did so as a different place, one more private and introspective.

A false restart occurred in 1977 with publication in *Quest* magazine of Johnson's design for a new house for David Whitney. Dubbed the Red House, it was planned for a site below the one now occupied by the architect's Study. Johnson presented the project as an ecological-mythological nest, discussing it as an odd mixture of mandalas, mysticism, and energy efficiency. Its stucco walls, painted barn-red, were to enclose a cloistered space, with a living area fourteen feet wide by thirty feet high. The intriguing design was never seen again, though its monastic leanings reemerged in Johnson's design for the Study when the architect returned to work in New Canaan in earnest in 1980.

In a different sense, however, 1977 was a banner year for The Glass House. That year, two essays appeared in *Oppositions*, one by Robert Stern and the other by Peter Eisenman, each reconsidering the design of The Glass House. *Oppositions* was the critical organ of the Institute of Architecture and Urban Studies, an architectural think tank devoted to contemporary architecture. Two years later, soon after Johnson turned up on the cover of *Time* magazine holding a model of his AT&T Building, the Institute hosted an exhibition covering that project and Johnson's Glass House, accompanied by a catalogue containing several scholarly treatments of Johnson's work. Among these was an essay, "The Glass House Revisited," by Kenneth Frampton.

Taken together, these three essays placed the origins of The Glass House at the center of a crucial debate in the late seventies over architecture's cultural role, a debate that sought to dictate architecture's immediate future. Eisenman, Stern, and Frampton used The Glass House to stake out three different positions that came to underpin most of the various trajectories followed by architecture in the United States in the 1980s.

Robert Stern, arch-postmodernist, disinterred Johnson's design sketches from the archives of The Museum of Modern Art, and discovered the aforementioned Syrian Arch scheme. Using it as the centerpiece of his concise "Evolution of Philip Johnson's Glass House, 1947–1948," Stern celebrated the eclecticism evident in the sketches in order to establish the central tenet of architectural postmodernism in America: that architectural design is a matter of style, not ideology. To make sure that the point was not lost, Stern repeated it three times in his six-paragraph essay.

Peter Eisenman, on the other hand, was keen to establish another position: that not only is architecture always ideological, but it is also irreducibly textual, that is, like a language, a source of rhetorical figures and metaphors. For Eisenman, the central issue for contemporary architecture is to take advantage of architecture's textuality to "write" alternatives to both humanism and modernism. In an extended meditation on Johnson's writings, Eisenman used Johnson's own words to argue that the architect cannot extricate his work from his words, that he cannot separate literary metaphors from architectural metaphors, and that he cannot isolate form, beauty, or experience from its cultural and political context, despite his heroic efforts to the contrary.

In the essay's climactic moment, Eisenman turned his attention toward the brick floor and fireplace of The Glass House, two elements that deviate markedly from Mies's Farnsworth House. Using Johnson's own explanation of the elements in his

1950 essay, Eisenman interprets them in a new light. Johnson had written: ". . . the cylinder made of the same brick as the platform from which it springs, forming the main motif of the house, was not derived from Mies, but rather from a burnt wooden village I once saw where nothing was left but the foundations and the chimneys of brick." From this statement, Eisenman suggested that The Glass House is nothing less than a monument to the horrors of war.

This elegant interpretation was a bit of a stretch, and Johnson pooh-poohed it immediately. But it could not be denied that the architect's odd wording called attention to itself. Throughout the United States, many had seen the remains of burnt houses where only a brick chimney was left standing. Indeed, such a ruin had existed near Johnson's New Canaan property at least since the 1950s. Why, then, did he refer to a "burnt wooden village"?

Kenneth Frampton entered the fray as the critic most committed to deriving a project for contemporary architecture from the formal, tectonic, and ideological principles of modernism, albeit one that would correct the movement's previous shortcomings. Since among modernism's conspicuous errors was its effort to erase architectural history, Frampton had to recuperate the status of architectural history within the modernist project. At the same time, he had to rebut Stern's reduction of that history to a question of style.

Frampton also had to counter Eisenman on at least one essential point. Eisenman's discussion of architecture as text and his consequent endorsement of Johnson's eclecticism ultimately threatened to deliver architectural design over to undisciplined play and to undermine its role as a decisive vehicle for political action. Though Eisenman argued that architecture was always ideological, he did not argue that it irrevocably installed one stable ideology, the necessary condition for Frampton's project to succeed. To the contrary, Eisenman's argument implied that such a goal for architecture was impossible to achieve. Thus, as Frampton turned his attention to The Glass House, it was inevitable that it would take the form of a comparison with Mies's Farnsworth House, a canonic work of modernism. Within the context of a debate on The Glass House, only by dint of that comparative study could the critic refute Stern and Eisenman and set in motion his project for a kinder, gentler modernism.

To establish his long-held doubts about the course of Johnson's digression from Mies, Frampton took the opportunity of his essay to reveal himself as the anonymous author of an assault on the Pavilion published sixteen years earlier in *Architectural Design*. Having set the record straight, he then undertook the most rigorous and learned consideration of The Glass House ever written.

He began his detailed study by tracing the formal transformations of the loggia belvedere from Schinkel through the early works of Mies to the Farnsworth House. He chose this strategy for several reasons. First of all, he convincingly demonstrated the historical development of the form of one of the most respected works of modernism. Thus he recovered the essential role of such studies to contemporary architecture without lapsing into the use of history as a source of stylistic quotation.

Second, he shifted the attention in the comparison between the two houses from the simple question of glass-walled architecture to the more complex question of the formal typology of transparency. Loggia and belvedere were two distinct devices, developed over centuries, by which architects introduced views of the exterior into a building. In these terms, a "glass house," whether by Mies or Johnson, is not a modern leap to something new, but an advanced stage in the development of a venerable formal problem.

In Frampton's view, Schinkel, one of the architects Johnson cites as an influence for his Glass House, initiated an effort to synthesize the loggia and belvedere. Frampton then showed that Mies took up that same synthetic project in his own work. Because glass can enclose while maintaining transparency, Mies was able to use the material to complete the synthesis. Beginning with the Barcelona pavilion, proceeding through the Tugendhat and Resor houses, Mies arrived at the final condensation in the Farnsworth House.

Moreover, by virtue of his coordinated use of material and construction methods—his tectonics—Mies was able to use that synthesis to achieve other efffects and advance other agendas. The tectonic expression of the Farnsworth House makes the formal synthesis clear while also frankly and honestly displaying the structure of the house, an effect devoutly desired by the modernists on moral grounds. Finally, the formal organization and tectonics of the Farnsworth House rendered its space continuous.

Taking this formal and tectonic history of the Farnsworth House as his basis, Frampton compared it to The Glass House. The developmental comparison is slightly askew, in that he treats the changes in the design of The Glass House evidenced in the MoMA sketches as equivalent to the changes in Mies's work over twenty years and through many completed projects.

Frampton arrived at three related conclusions. First: ". . . where Mies is always tectonic, Johnson is invariably scenographic." One of the key examples here is a comparison between Johnson's chair bar, the so-called wainscot, and a similar element in Mies's Tugendhat. While the former is painted black, thus blending into the structural system, though it is not a structural element, the latter is rendered materially distinct from the structure. Though Frampton saw the stylistic advantage of Johnson's decision and commended it as such, it is, nevertheless, an impugning observation, at least in terms of the tectonic morality of modernism.

Second, Frampton found The Glass House developmentally naïve when compared to the evolution leading to the Farnsworth House. Of course, it is only naïve if the formal issues arising in Mies's work, such as the loggia/belvedere synthesis, are taken as the standard of sophistication. As Robert Vuyosevich argued in his 1992 comparison of the two houses, if the standard is taken to be Semper's archetype of the domestic house, it is the Farnsworth House that falls short.

Finally, Frampton argued that the phenomenological impact of The Glass House—that is, its finite, domestic space—derived from its suppression of the structural system. Johnson terminated the roof plane at the corner column, turning the house into a beautifully detailed, but closed, box. The effect was amplified when Johnson painted the structural system black and set it flush with the glass walls. To the contrary, Mies cantilevered the roof beyond the columns and expressed the structural system by painting it white and detaching it from the glass walls. Thus Mies's space, sandwiched between the roof and floor, flows past the glass, through the structure and beyond. Moreover, in the Farnsworth House one sees the shadow of the structure on the glass, a confirmation of its distinct presence.

From these three points, Frampton judged that The Glass House was a bourgeois work, "a solipsism raised to unparal-

leled elegance." In sum, his brilliant erudition simply confirmed what Johnson had claimed he was doing all along. In fact, in a 1976 television interview with Rosamond Bernier, Johnson made many of the same points as Frampton, though in somewhat more accessible terms. The only difference, in the end, was Frampton's political interpretation, which Johnson rejected, but never contested.

Indeed, concerned that the political implications of his formal and tectonic analysis might not carry the same persuasive force for others that it did for himself, Frampton abandoned his scholarly rigor at the last moment and resorted to Eisenman's metaphorical reading of the brick chimney. But in an act of critical desperation, Frampton turned Eisenman's suggestion into an assumed historical fact, writing that the "ruin in question was almost certainly the blitz-krieged remains of a village." Given his difficulty here in putting forward a convincing statement of his project in its own terms, perhaps it is not altogether surprising that, in the next decade, Stern's and Eisenman's theoretical projects flourished while Frampton's neomodernist project struggled to survive.

Though he began sketching new additions to the estate in 1977, Johnson did not actually build there again until he erected his Study in 1980. Then, in short order, he began work on the Chain-Link House and the Lincoln Kirstein Tower, finishing both in 1985. Still on the drawing board is an Entry Tower, to be used as a visitors' center when the estate is taken over by the National Trust. Designed but as yet unbuilt is a garden slat house, to be located across Ponus Ridge Road, next to a second home owned by David Whitney. Though the slat house, like the heather garden, is not part of the estate proper, its proximity to The Glass House and its design character make it worthy of consideration.

In siting, form, and program, this group is quite different from Johnson's previous work in New Canaan, more intimate, more contemplative. In them, one sees most clearly Johnson the collector and Johnson the diarist, for in each, one finds a personal meditation on issues arising in contemporary architecture. The stark, white Study sits alone in a field far south of The Glass House, unconnected by any path; to get to it, Johnson must walk through the grass. Its object-in-a-park siting recalls a Corbusian theme, while its form reflects both on Le Corbusier's elemental geometries and, more particularly, on Rossi's reassembly of those elements into icons of architectural memory.

For years, Johnson used the Sculpture Gallery as his office; the Study is his retreat from the relentless vastness of that space. In it, the architect surrenders to his desire for a womblike, monastic enclosure. Within the thickened walls, lit by an overhead oculus and single rectangular window, he reads and works on his designs, surrounded by shelves of books tabbed with hundreds of yellow slips, mostly marking his favorite architectural images.

The completion of the Library led to a visit to the estate by the noted Italian architectural critic and historian Francesco Dal Co. The critic was the first to view Johnson as essentially a collector and the estate as an extension of his collecting activities more obviously expressed through the art. In his essay for *Lotus*, Dal Co traces the philosophical and autobiographical implications of Johnson' collecting. His dense but beautifully wrought argument turns on the Study. Had the critic visited a year earlier, it is unlikely that his thoughts would have moved in the same direction.

On the other hand, when Vincent Scully revisited The Glass House in 1986, after the Chain-Link House and Kirstein Tower were finished, the work he liked least was the Study. In his essay for *Architectural Digest*, he dismissed the white specter, finding it adrift, even sinister. No doubt this was due in large part to the fact that the mythophilic critic could not find any hint of prehistory in its form, which he could only manage to trace through Rossi back to Boullée. If Scully had taken a second look, he might have seen a *trullo*, a whitewashed, cone-roofed building-type unique to the Puglia region of Italy, thought to have originated during the Stone Age. Perhaps then he would have found more solace in these ancient roots.[2]

Scully was also cool toward the Chain-Link House, finding it somewhat morbid. Not far from the Study, and built to protect the lily gardens from ravenous deer, the garden folly was Johnson's marriage of Robert Venturi to Frank Gehry. In a scheme for Franklin Park in Philadelphia, Venturi resurrected a ghost of Benjamin Franklin's house, drawing it in three dimensions with steel I-beams painted white. Likewise, with the Chain-Link House, Johnson resurrected a ghost over the exposed foundations of a farm building long gone. Unlike Venturi, however, Johnson rendered the structure in chain-link and split it down the middle, *à la* Gehry. The house lacks the wit of Venturi and the clash of Gehry; it is, however, far more elegant than the work of either of these architects. "That," Johnson quips, only half jokingly, "is why mine is so much better than theirs."

Because of its operating cost, Johnson removed the fountain from the pond in 1977. In so doing, however, he lost a key landscaping device, a vertical element delimiting the extension of the space from The Glass House across the valley. The architect finally replaced that important element with the concrete-block tower. Because of its spatial function and its relationship to the pond and Pavilion, the tower's location is less improvisational than that of either the Study or the Chain-Link House. However, it is an equally personal work, as different from the public ostentation of the fountain as the Study is from the Sculpture Gallery. Only one at a time can mount the tower to enjoy its dra-

matic view; that is, if one is willing to dare the precarious climb, Johnson's tongue-in-cheek grudge against handrails.

The Tower is dedicated to a friend, Lincoln Kirstein. In collaboration with George Balanchine, Kirstein founded the New York City Ballet; later, he became the company's general director. He and Johnson formed a close friendship while the architect was designing the New York State Theater at Lincoln Center, home of the New York City Ballet.

Scully was particularly attracted to the Kirstein Tower, seeing in it Gothic ruins and Escher's staircases. As well, the Tower appears a fragmented and reflected collage of the New York City skyline. Such an interpretation not only connects its design to architectural themes current at the time, but also lends another meaning to the difficult climb to the top.

Though the Entry Tower/Visitors' Center and slat house are not yet built, the issues at work in their design are clear. In the Entry Tower, Johnson is experimenting with design themes that came to his attention during his work on the Deconstructivist Architecture exhibition at MoMA in 1988. In its current version, a brick L-shaped wall, a copper-clad wing-shaped wall, and a tilted roof are sewn together by a staircase into an incommensurate assembly. Though the visitors'-center program makes the Entry Tower the most public of the late works, Johnson stacks the functions and scales the Tower down to reduce as far as possible the institutionality of its space.

With the slat house, Johnson turns his mind toward the complex geometric solids that have recently replaced angles, shards, and fragments in contemporary design. In it, the architect subtends one-eighth of a sphere with a right-angled wall. The graceful form is constructed out of slats of wooden lath, aligned vertically on the right-angled wall and horizontally on the curve to produce intricate interference patterns on the exterior and similar light-and-shadow effects in the interior.

Though these late works greatly expand the space of the estate, even carrying past its proper boundaries, they do so in an *ad hoc* fashion. For the most part, they are local affairs, whose connections to the major works on the property are informal, incidental, or even nonexistent. They do not serve any overarching concept; nevertheless, they knit a new cohesion.

To grasp that cohesion, we must return almost to the beginning one last time, to pick up the threads of a pattern. After Johnson finished the original scheme, many critics declared its triangular plan decisive and final. The claim of finality was repeated, though in different terms, after the pond group transformed The Glass House into an English garden estate. When Robert Hughes visited, he announced that the Sculpture Gallery was the finishing touch. Even Francesco Dal Co, who saw Johnson's property as an open-ended col-

lection, could not resist the feeling that the most recent addition—in his case, the Study—completed the collection. Over the course of the estate's transformations, critics have treated each new addition as the consummate final touch.

In truth, though The Glass House has never been complete, neither has it ever been incomplete! Like an American city, it has expanded, not according to a master plan, but by annexation and diverse development. Each addition of land and building has transformed it from one whole to another. For that reason, despite the multiplicity of its organizations and the variety of its forms, styles, and materials, there is nothing eclectic about the Johnson estate. Like The Glass House itself, it is an amalgam of disjoint components into a remarkable organic unity, endlessly capable of growth, that at the same time celebrates the differences among its parts.

In the current cultural context, to unfold the possiblilities of an organization whose coherence evolves more from its components' distinctions than from their similarities would seem to be among the most absorbing reasons to visit New Canaan. Yet, as for any great work of art, as the context changes, so, too, do the meanings the work engenders. Thus, although we conclude this particular exploration, let us resist the impression that we have seen the final development or written the final word on the architect's estate. After all, for over forty years, Philip Johnson's clearest message has been simply this: we can add to but never complete the catalogue of the incidental effects of a glass house.

Notes
1. Following Johnson, I will, on occasion, use the name Glass House to refer both to the house itself and to the complex as a whole.
2. I am indebted to Professor Douglas Graf for this observation.

Philip Johnson
The Glass House

Arthur Drexler

From Interiors & Industrial Design, *October 1949*

Architecture Opaque and Transparent

In order to live successfully in Philip Johnson's new house one would have to be Philip Johnson, or at least a reasonable facsimile. In its time Versailles must also have been a little problematic, to the peasants outside, but after one has admitted that several Louis's were able to stand the pace without undue strain, one is free to enjoy the architecture.

Out in New Canaan, in the soft summertime, the trees wave in the ambient air and the grass grows with a fresh, poetic abundance. On a shelf of this good land Mr. Johnson has placed two large pieces of furniture. One is a brick box and the other is a glass cage. In due time a pool of sand containing a statue, perhaps by Maillol, will be set between these separate buildings.

The site itself has been used as a room whose natural boundaries, though vague and shifting, according to the seasons, are nevertheless constant walls. On the east a screen of trees conceals the vast room within from the public road. Then the land slopes down past the guest house to a broad, clear lawn, with the glass pavilion placed at its western limit. Immediately beyond the house is an abrupt drop into a valley, out of which appear only the trimmed tops of trees. Though each of the buildings has a distinct object relation to the landscape, certain parts of the architecture register more clearly than others as furnishings one might expect to find in a room. Thus the site—a huge hall with a green-growing floor—has had carpets (not houses) carefully spread out on it. The largest carpet is the brick platform of the main house, and in appearance the roof and four glass walls which happen to protect it are of comparatively minor importance.

The brick used on the platform is laid in a herringbone pattern, and, as elsewhere in the house, is Pennsylvania Ironspot. Its color ranges from a deep, orange-flecked red to dark brown, and it has been heavily glazed with wax to bring out a cold, purple overtone.

The platform supports only one object which rises to the full height of the room. This is a chubby brick cylinder ten feet in diameter. Besides containing the fireplace and the bathroom, it appears to be a heavy, solid object, like a paperweight, holding the platform to the ground. Its round mass thickens the space around it, congesting attention at the fireplace.

The roof, and the steel columns by which it is supported, are dropped over the platform like the kind of glass bell used to protect Victorian clocks. However, the roof, far from being rounded, is a perfectly flat slab with a hole in it, through which projects the brick cylinder. Its reappearance on top of the house emphasizes the relative weightlessness of the steel cage, and also allows the chimney to be incorporated within an unbroken shape.

Both the floor and the ceiling are radiant heated. The furnace is located in the guest house across the lawn, and from there the pipes move out under the gravel path towards the glass pavilion. With the top and bottom of the house radiating heat, the room temperature has reached a

tropical 109° in the middle of winter. When that happens the four doors are left open. At the beginning of cold weather, when the heating unit is turned on, there is a slight loss of heat to the ground which the coils must cross to reach the main house. But the ground itself quickly warms up, blanketing the coils in the heat they radiate. And as the pipes run under the gravel path, they automatically melt the snow, keeping the path clear all winter.

In plan the house is a rectangle 32'x56'. The long dimension is divided into three equal bays, and the steel columns are placed to emphasize the extremities of the total volume. The height from floor to finished ceiling is 10'-6", with a door rising uninterrupted to the full height on each facade; a simple enough way to establish the grandiose scale.

All the furniture in the glass house was designed by Mies van der Rohe. In the living area a sand-colored carpet, like a raft in the ocean, provides safe passage for a low couch, two of the famous chairs designed originally for the German Pavilion in the 1929 Barcelona Fair, a glass and metal coffee table which first appeared in the Tugendhat house, and an elegant leather-cushioned stool. Each of these modern classics is placed with a meticulous precision equivalent to that which went into its design. The arrangement is so completely and irrevocably formal that, far from freezing people, it frees people from the need to be formal.

The fact that the doors are arranged

on a double axis, with the columns symmetrically aligned, and that the floor is in effect a modified podium (the steps have been eliminated) suggests a highly refined and metallic Greek temple.

This classical reference is strengthened by the purely negative character of the space between the columns. The facades, entirely of glass, are the minimum interference between the area they enclose and the surrounding view. Because the individual panels of glass are so large, interest is automatically shifted away from the glass itself to the divisions made by the steel columns. But when the sun splashes through the trees, the glass and the house with it seem to disappear in a reflected mobile of foliage and clouds. Protection from this sometimes dazzling barrage of sunlight is achieved without benefit of curtains. There are 176 feet of glass wall, which, if curtained, would have made the room resemble the inside of a ballerina's skirt. Rather than this, each wall of the room has been equipped with a set of pandanus cloth shades. These are like flat, narrow scrolls, permanently unrolled. They can be spread out to cover a long expanse of glass, or banked one behind the other, by sliding them along a track in the ceiling.

The house is well equipped with electric lights, but for no reason other than that it is sometimes absolutely necessary to see what one is doing. At night the interior is lighted entirely by a huge candelabra and the fireplace. Outdoors, however, concealed spotlights wash the landscape in a

soft glow, so that the room within is surrounded by an illuminated wall of trees. This light is not designed to effect a transition from indoors to outdoors, but rather to completely reverse the order of the two kinds of space. A Poussin painting on a metal easel, near the cluster of chairs, is set just where the conventional might have placed an abstraction. By a fortunate arrangement between the architect and the landscape, the trees outside now resemble those in the painting, where they look like feathers stuck in the ground.

A spotlight on the painting provides a third source of light within the room, but without undoing the mood of baronial splendor established by the high fireplace and the candelabra. The latter is made of two iron hoops painted black, one on the floor, one in mid-air. They are connected to each other by a thin rod, and the top rim is crowned by eleven candles in small glass cups. At night reflections of this curiously medieval piece of equipment are repeated indefinitely in each of the glass walls, until they vanish in some mysterious black forest beyond.

There are only two major area divisions in the entire room. The most important, in terms of the amount of space it conceals, is the line of cabinets marking off the bedroom. These cabinets are only six feet high, and the basic shape of the house is maintained because it is possible to see the intersection of ceiling and glass wall behind them. At the other end of the room a statue by Elie Nadelman serves as a minor punctuation of space, much the way the freestanding Poussin landscape does. The statue's soft contours contrast agreeably with the clean lines of the house, while its decorative curves blend with the tapestry of trees outside.

The other major division in the living area, aside from the brick cylinder, is the long line of 42″ high cabinets which contains the kitchen. Two panels on top of this unit, when opened and folded back, provide a black linoleum work surface. The sink, two refrigerators, a stove, and storage are all included in the one unit, besides a liquor closet which opens into the living area. With ventilation from all four sides, and in a room as large as this—the whole house is one room—cooking odors disappear almost immediately. Six spotlights above provide light, and a rubber mat on the floor behind the counter simplifies the mopping-up activities. The dignified proportions of this counter effectively transform it from a mere work space to the scene of pontifical ceremonies. The mixing of a gin and tonic, or the scrambling of eggs, becomes a luxury which is the significant blend of ritual and necessity.

The glass house is the most economical expression of a volume, in terms of the architectural apparatus used. In fact it is less like a house than like a diagram drawn in the air to indicate a quantity of space. The transparent volume thus described by its walls and columns might almost have been lifted out and set over on the other side of the lawn, where it suddenly solidi-

fied into the massive and opaque guest house. In this building another attitude towards the life one ought to live inside a house, though not necessarily an opposing one, has been thoroughly accounted for. When one is tired of moving in a schematically indicated volume, one adjourns to the neighboring block of closet-like rooms. The guest house contains, besides a kitchen, bathroom, and utility room, a study, an art gallery, and two bedrooms. The walls inside are plaster, painted white, with a bank of closets in both bedrooms painted dark grey. Here, as in the glass house, all the doors rise to the full ceiling height. The bedrooms and the study, arranged in a line at the back of the building, each have a single window. This is a porthole in a wood frame, five feet in diameter, hinged at the bottom and opening into the room. These round windows, seen from the outside, stress the continuous brick surface of the building. From within they are (after a moment or two) less noticeable than a right-angled window might be. But their chief merit is that it is more interesting to look at them than through them. The art gallery, the kitchen, and the bathroom have skylights, but there are no other windows in the building. This proves that under certain circumstances the attractiveness of a house can be gauged according to its resemblance to a prison, and the guest house is a restful place.

The view-stopping quality of its opaque walls stands in relation to the glass pavilion much as do the brick cylinder and the Nadelman statue. But where these two solid units screen and define areas of interest and movement within-doors, the guest house performs this function in the larger architecture which includes the landscape itself.

The units of form which have been combined to make up each of the two houses are plainly derived from construction techniques. Logically, the refinement of each of these details leads to a more precise and direct statement of the building processes involved, and thus to a better architecture. In both of these houses it is this straightforward attitude towards building which, at first sight, appears to have shaped their design. But in any style, even one in which details of function are joyously proclaimed to the world, only certain things are selected to be shown. The intersection of post and beams at the corners, for example, is made overpoweringly clear, but a detail of equal significance, like the unlovely metal construction in the roof, has been carefully hidden under a flat, plaster ceiling, like a huge window shade pulled over something slightly embarrassing. This fine discrimination between things to be shown and things not to be shown is what constitutes a style. In this case the style is a romantic one. It begins with the problems of building but soon moves on to more important things, including among them a series of allusions to other styles. Poussin, who lived and painted in Italy most of his life, developed his own version of classicism. He ranged his figures, which resembled Greek statues, parallel to the picture plane, tightened his color schemes, balanced each element for its greatest formal impact, and elaborated several other devices which were all part of a classic conception of art. The reason for all this was a desire to give a more enduring substance to what motivated him in the first place, namely, a fascination with the paraphernalia of antiquity. What once captivated Poussin may now leave most people less than indifferent, but the formal perfection of his art endures. It also suggests that "purism," when caught up in a larger form, means pure romanticism.

Philip Johnson

From Architectural Review, *September 1950 (Volume 108, Number 645)*

House at New Canaan, Connecticut

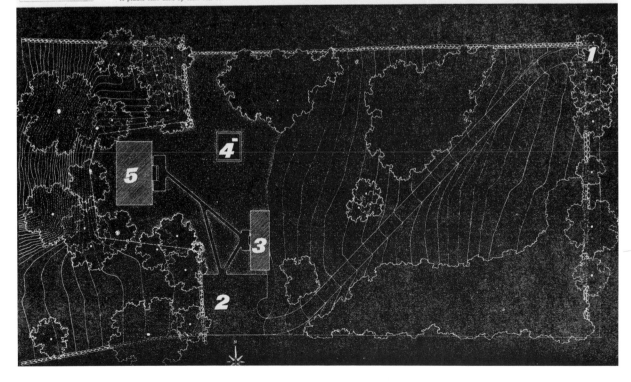

HOUSE AT NEW CANAAN, CONNECTICUT

PHILIP JOHNSON: ARCHITECT

The latest development in 'skin and bones' architecture* is Philip Johnson's glass house, which he has designed for his own occupation. Since the work is proclaimed by the architect as frankly derivative, in this publication of it and the adjacent guest building, Mr. Johnson has followed the unusual and, it should be granted, praiseworthy expedient of revealing the sources of his inspiration. These are presented in consecutive order, and precede the illustrations of the two houses. The commentary is Philip Johnson's own.

* A phrase once used by Mies van der Rohe to describe the structural system of which he is the leading exponent.

key to site plan 1. entrance to site. 2. car park. 3. guest house. 4. sculpture. 5. glass house.

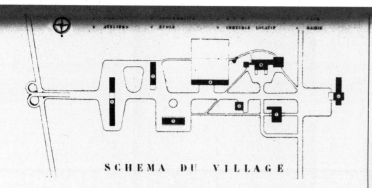

SCHEMA DU VILLAGE

1 Le Corbusier: Farm Village Plan—1933.

The approach to the house through meadow and copse is derived from English Eighteenth Century precedent. The actual model is Count Pückler's estate at Muskau in Silesia. The driveway is straight, however, like the pathways in the plan above. The footpath pattern between the two houses I copied from the spiderweb-like forms of Le Corbusier, who delicately runs his communications without regard for the axis of his buildings or seemingly for any kind of pattern.

2 Mies van der Rohe: Ideal arrangement of Illinois Institute of Technology Buildings, 1939.

The arrangement of the two buildings and the statue group is influenced by Mies' theory of organizing buildings in a group. The arrangement is rectilinear but the shapes tend to overlap and slide by each other in an asymmetric manner.

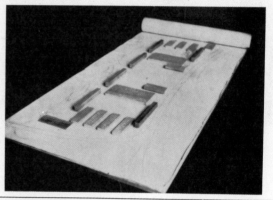

THÉO VAN DOESBURG
GENERALBASS DER MALEREI

3 Theo Van Doesburg: The Basso Continuo of Painting. (Published in "G" an *avant garde* magazine by Mies van der Rohe in 1922).

The idea of asymmetric sliding rectangles was furthest developed in the De Stijl aesthetics of war-time Holland. These shapes, best known to posterity through the painting of the late Piet Mondrian, still have an enormous influence on many other architects besides myself.

4 Plan and Perspective of the Acropolis at Athens from Choisy: *L'Histoire de l'Art Grecque.*

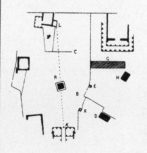

Choisy proved that the Greeks restricted the angle of approach to their buildings to the oblique; also that they placed their monuments so that only one major building dominated the field of vision from any given point.
The grouping of my buildings follows Choisy: from the focal point at the beginning of the footpath near the parking lot, the brick house (Propylaea) is passed and forms a wall on the right hand. The statue group (Athene Promachos) is in full view slightly to the right. The glass house comes into view (from an oblique angle) only after the pine tree at the angle of the promontory is circumnavigated.

arl Friedrich Schinkel: Casino in Glienicke Park near Potsdam c. 1830. Entrance façade.

6 Karl Friedrich Schinkel: Casino in Glienicke Park near Potsdam c. 1830. Terrace overlooking the Havel.

The site relation of my house is pure Neo-Classic Romantic— more specifically, Schinkelesque. Like his Casino my house is approached on dead-level and, like his, faces its principal (rear) façade toward a sharp bluff.

The Eighteenth Century preferred more regular sites than this and the Post-Romantic Revivalists preferred hill tops to the cliff edges or shelves of the Romantics (Frank Lloyd Wright, that great Romantic, prefers shelves or hillsides).

Claude Nicholas Ledoux: Maison des Gardes Agricoles, at Maupertuis c. 1780.

8 Mies van der Rohe: Farnsworth House, 1947. (Now under construction near Chicago).

The cubic, "absolute" form of my glass house, and the separation of functional units into two absolute shapes rather than a major and minor massing of parts comes directly from Ledoux, the Eighteenth Century father of modern architecture. (See Emil Kaufmann's excellent study Von Ledoux bis Le Corbusier.) The cube and the sphere, the pure mathematical shapes, were dear to the hearts of those intellectual revolutionaries from the Baroque, and we are their descendants.

The idea of a glass house comes from Mies van der Rohe. Mies had mentioned to me as early as 1945 how easy it would be to build a house entirely of large sheets of glass. I was sceptical at the time, and it was not until I had seen the sketches of the Farnsworth House that I started the three-year work of designing my glass house. My debt is therefore clear, in spite of obvious difference in composition and relation to the ground.

Philip Johnson

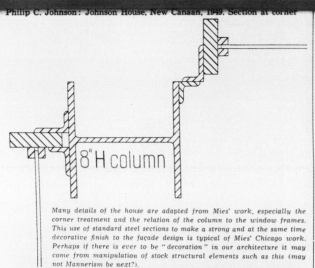

8" H column

Many details of the house are adapted from Mies' work, especially the corner treatment and the relation of the column to the window frames. This use of standard steel sections to make a strong and at the same time decorative finish to the façade design is typical of Mies' Chicago work. Perhaps if there is ever to be "decoration" in our architecture it may come from manipulation of stock structural elements such as this (may not Mannerism be next?).

10 Kasimir Malevitch: Suprematist Element: Circle—1913.

Although I had forgotten the Malevitch picture, it is obviously the inspiration for the plan of the glass house. Malevitch proved what interesting sur-rounding areas could be created by correctly placing a circle in a rectangle. Abstract painting of forty years ago remains even today the strongest single aesthetic influence on the grammar of architecture.

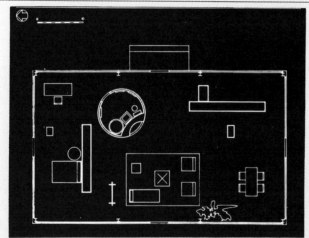

11 Johnson House: Plan of Glass Unit.

North end, sleeping and writing; brick cylinder, washing and w.c.; south-east, cooking; south-west, eating; west, sitting

Except for the cylinder, the plan of the house is Miesian. The use of 6 foot closets to divide yet unite space is his. The grouping of the furniture asymmetrically around a coffee table is his. The relation of cabinets to the cylinder, however, is more "painterly" than Mies would sanction.

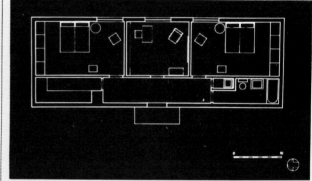

12 Johnson House: Plan of Brick Unit.

Two double guests' bedrooms with study between; combined entrance hall-picture gallery with storage room at one end, bathroom and shower at the other.

The guest house with Baroque plan central corridor and three symmetrically placed rooms, was derived from Mies' designs. The three round windows in the rear of the façade are a Renaissance approach to a Miesian motif. Mies uses the round window as a method of admitting light in a long brick wall in a manner least to disturb the continuity of the wall. A rectangular hole would compete in direction with the shape of the wall itself. I used the round windows for the same reason, with a totally different compositional effect.

13. Johnson House: North End of West Wall.

The multiple reflections on the 18' pieces of plate glass, which seem superimposed on the view through the house, help give the glass a type of solidity; a direct Miesian aim which he expressed twenty-five years ago: "I discovered by working with actual glass models that the important thing is the play of reflections and not the effect of light and shadow as in ordinary buildings."

14 Johnson House: General View of Brick and Glass Units.

The bi-axial symmetry of each façade of the glass house is as absolute as Ledoux and much purer than any Baroque example. Opposite sides of my house are identical and the "minor" axis is almost as developed as the "major". (Is there a slight left-over of Baroque in the fact that the front door is in the long elevation?)

15 Johnson House: Entrance Façade of Glass Unit.

16 Johnson House: Entrance Façade of Brick Unit.

The guest house with central door and severely axial plan is jointly descended from the Baroque and from designs by Mies. (See 12.)

17 Johnson House: Glass Unit at Night.

The cylinder, made of the same brick as the plat-form from which it springs, forming the main motif of the house, was not derived from Mies, but rather from a burnt wooden village I saw once where nothing was left but foundations and chimneys of brick. Over the chimney I slipped a steel cage with a glass skin. The chimney forms the anchor.

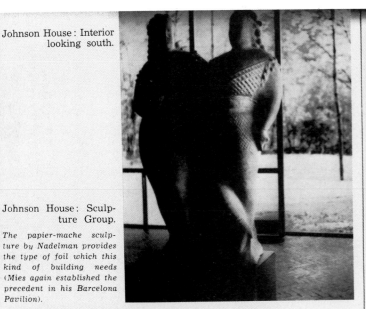

Johnson House: Interior looking south.

Johnson House: Sculpture Group.

The papier-mache sculpture by Nadelman provides the type of foil which this kind of building needs (Mies again established the precedent in his Barcelona Pavilion).

20 Johnson House: Interior looking west.

The view of the valley, with its repoussoir of giant trees, is contrived with the aid of many Baroque landscapes. A view without a frame seems impossible after the Seventeenth Century.

Johnson House: Cooking Unit.

The kitchen I reduced to a simple bar so that it would not close off any space. I have no idea what precedent I followed on that.

22 Johnson House: Interior, north-east corner.

Bed and writing desk, with strips of pandanus cloth hanging from the ceiling—the only screening I felt to be necessary.

(See photograph on page 38.) Mies van der Rohe has not only influenced the concept of the house. He has designed all of the furniture—some of it a quarter century ago, none of it later than 1930.

Philip Johnson

From Perspecta 7, *1961*

"Johnson"

Perspecta 7 *is a key document of the second generation of the Modern Movement's International Style as it came to be practiced in America. As such, it can be regarded as the formalist counterpart to the socio-functionalist* Team Ten Primer. Perspecta 7 *not only contains innovative work by principal form-givers of the day—including John Johansen, Louis Kahn, Paul Rudolph, and Eero Saarinen, as well as Johnson—but also carries with it critical assessments of their work, and of the then-current situation in American architecture, written by journalists and historians (Peter Collins, Walter McQuade, and Sibyl Moholy-Nagy), as well as two provocative views of American practice by English architects then little known to American readers, James Gowan and Colin St. John Wilson.*

In Perspecta 7, *Johnson is represented by some of his most daring if unresolved work of mid-career, including the miniaturized pavilion for his garden at New Canaan, and projects for the Benedictine Priory at Washington, D.C., and the Sheldon Memorial Art Gallery, Lincoln, Nebraska. The text, which the editors title with ironic equivocation simply "Johnson," needs little comment. What does bear remarking upon is Johnson's relationship to* Perspecta, The Yale Architectural Journal, *an occasional publication edited by the architectural students at Yale, which he has supported to the fullest extent since its inception under the patronage of George Howe in 1951. Johnson has reserved for* Perspecta's *pages some of his most interesting buildings and projects and some of his most carefully articulated essays about architecture. In the 1950's, when he was a pivotal figure on the Yale scene, he participated in the after-hours discussions organized by the students. Some of these sessions were tape-recorded, transcribed, and collated to constitute a "conversation" with other key figures, notably Louis Kahn and Vincent Scully, and published in* Perspecta 2 *as "On the Responsibility of the Architect." In* Perspecta 1, *Johnson, along with Buckminster Fuller and Paul Rudolph, was singled out as a representative of "New Directions" in architecture.* Perspecta 3 *contains his "Seven Crutches of Modern Architecture," as well as a presentation of his Wiley House, accompanied by a brief essay by him*

explaining the house. Perspecta 7 *includes the material in this section.* Perspecta 9/10 *was privileged to benefit from Johnson's generosity to what had by then become an established, if erratic, publishing venture. Not only did he write "on commission"— and, of course, without fee—the essay, "Whence and Whither" (see pp. 27–32), but he also permitted me, its editor, to rummage through his files and select a number of hitherto unpublished and unbuilt designs that I was anxious to present in order to "flesh out" the story of his struggle against the formal straitjacket of the orthodox International Style—a story I then regarded and continue to regard as critical to setting the scene for the emerging style which has since come to be described as post-Modernism.*

Robert A. M. Stern

In an intellectual atmosphere of casual heaviness in design, of careful not-design, or at least a look of to-hell-with-it, it is difficult to write of my work. It seems I cannot but be Classically inspired; symmetry, order, clarity above all. I cannot throw around cardboard boxes, or make a pseudo-functional arrangement of air-conditioning ducts into a *trouvé*'d type of design.

In the opposite direction, I can no longer build glass boxes—the pleasant glass box for all uses!!—the general purpose universal box. We live in another era.

Like the old Beaux-Arts men in my youth, yearning for their *partis* and *entourages*, I now look back with pleasure, and yes, even some nostalgia, on the days in the twenties when the battle line was clear, the modern versus the eclectic, the dreams of universal panaceas, standards, types, norms, that would "solve" architecture.

Now we know that we cannot "solve" anything. The only principle that I can conceive of believing in is the Principle of Uncertainty. It is a brave architect that can possess convictions and beliefs, and keep his tongue out of his cheek. Personally, my desire for order and clarity will have to suffice. I cannot find any shapes to copy, and forms like the good old Malevitch or Mondrian 1920 ones to fit in. Nor do my contemporaries give me a clear lead. The very best known of my own generation do one building in one day and the very opposite the next. It has got so that a critic can hardly say "This must be a Zilch building; it has the earmarks of his style or manner." We seem, even more than ever in that much maligned 19th century, to be making a new architecture every day. Where are we at?

My own manner is in these three buildings. It seems an architect is only inarticulate about his own work. It is much easier to write about Saarinen and Rudolph than about Johnson. I really don't know why I designed these the way I did. Others will tell me.

The three projects represent two poles of my present tendencies. The clearest and furthest developed (the Pavilion is under way) is the direction of the Pavilion and the Sheldon Art Gallery. It is clear from the pictures that the grammar is the same, the buildings only are different; one is symmetrical with infill—making pilasters out of the columns. (How long ago it was that Goethe said the pilaster is a lie! One would answer him today—"yes, but what a delightfully useful one.") The other is sporty, open, and only hiddenly symmetrical. One is hand-carved travertine, the other precast concrete.

The grammar is rather Classical and yet the idea of it came from looking at the Delaunay St. Séverin series. His toed-in Gothic arcade suggested the widened bases. The concave sides of the columns came from the wish to vault in four directions without the use of imposts or soffits. Also a High Gothic wish. The problem, as usual, was the corner column. A concave curve at the cornice was unthinkable, so it is convex, warping toward the typical concave base. The arch itself is a hit-or-miss ellipse, created freehand, and calculated afterward. The modularity, so un-Baroque, is probably modern. (Greek revival modularity is usually strengthened at the corners, this is not.)

The importance of the Sheldon Art Gallery lies in the central court which divides the functions into four clear spaces and itself forming the fifth; the Grand Salon, the stairwell within, focuses all the subsidiary spaces. This focus is intended to destroy museum fatigue at the same time giving a lift to the spirits. The coffered ceiling "vaulting," again carved travertine, should make a monumental room. (Classical or neo-Gothic?)

The Pavilion is a sport. First, it is underscaled. Each square unit which appears first to be scaled at 12 × 12 feet is in actuality only 8 × 8. The idea is to make giants of the visitor (an idea borrowed from the dwarfs' chambers in Mantua). The intention is to place underscaled concrete furniture within some units. The central little pool (higher than the surrounding pond) with its radiating canals is a barrier from unit to unit and at the same time an accented feature. The water from the canals falls on thin metal, to tinkle gently. The ceilings which look 9 feet high are 6 feet, very unsettling. A hundred-foot-high *jet d'eau* will play in the pond in full view.

The design is aimed at the amusement we all feel of the miniature and the complicated; the pleasure of hiding among a forest of columns (Córdoba?); the sense that one of us is in one pavilion and can't reach the other except by a long circumambulation; the feeling of an island and the little pool on the little island.

The composition itself is a casual assembly of squares, roofed, open, or water, the roofed elements being symmetrically laid out. Again there is no Baroque accent, hence quite "modern," but certainly not Chinese in spite of the moon-viewing im-

plications. It merely seemed to me as I was working on the design that architecture has room for pleasure domes, even if somewhat reduced in scale.

The Benedictine Priory is something else again. It is certainly historical in plan—a narrow, long and high (90 foot) barrel-vaulted basilica, sans transept. But it is also purely functional since the shape was developed originally for conventual liturgy. Why change? This is the very tradition (along with the Gregorian chant) that must be preserved in the architecture. But the preservation of the shape—the processional length, the height, need not interfere with contemporary forms and materials. It is to be concrete—*béton brut* throughout, columns, buttresses, infill and vault. The walls are partly vertical, partly canted, depending on whether they follow the column or the buttress. Both column and buttress are *plissé*; that is V's of thin concrete, and the buttresses alternate with rather than support the columns. The cross section is rather like a gantry crane. The indescribable terminations of the nave and apse are flat and should be stained glass, but only dimly translucent, since the main light source comes from skylights on the side aisles, which wash the walls. There is no light directly into the chancel.

The competition for the Idlewild Union Air Terminal, which I lost to I. M. Pei, is more or less in line with the Benedictine Priory. Like the column sequences there, the column clusters are the main point of the design, making humanly apprehendable spaces out of a building, which, because of the program, was very, very long—1,100 feet. The main problem was the very low ceiling necessary for so large a room—47 feet. To make it seem higher, rather than using a 12-foot-deep truss lowering the ceiling to 35 feet, we (Lev Zetlin, engineer) developed a sine curve, double-waving roof, emphasizing, like the column clusters, the eleven bays. The design of the façade of each bay is symmetrical and classically or Classically mounted: The ground floor, solid stone, with the door in the middle; a glazed *piano nobile*; small panes of glass with heavy mullions turning at 45° at the cornice line where the roof dips. The feature of the exterior (impossible to draw) is the 35-foot overhang.

The plan is different from most new airports in that the de-planing passenger proceeds through the Great Room to buses or taxis. It is the fashion today not to allow de-planing and en-planing passengers to mix. I am glad the genius who designed the Grand Central Station lets me come from the train into the same Great Room where others are about to en-train. What good is a great gateway room if the visitor is not to see it?

The great airport of our age has yet to be designed. Forty-seven feet high is the limit at Idlewild. In the cause of sacred monumentality, we should get up a public subscription to raise the height of the Idlewild central tower, which controls the height of all the buildings of the group. Why should the air age not have the glow of the Renaissance Age? The Grand Central and the Pennsylvania Station, before they fell on evil days, were spaces that made the heart sing, spaces that never got too small as traffic expanded, as do our airports. What we have lost is a public passion for greatness. No cathedrals? Not even any great public nuclear plant? What is our generation going vicariously to enjoy as in old days the palace, the church, or the Acropolis? We cannot all of us enjoy slum clearance and parking lots.

The questions are rhetorical. There are no answers. A culture gets the monuments it desires.

Philip Johnson

From Show *magazine, III, June 1963*

Full Scale False Scale

Johnson's garden folly is considered by many critics to mark the nadir of his "ballet school" phase. The pavilion does not seem to satisfy: not because it is frivolous, but because it is not frivolous enough; not because it is a rich man's plaything, but because the rich man was not rich enough, using earnest pre-cast concrete where only either lath and plaster or marble would do. Johnson's essay, on the other hand, is rather a different matter. It does convince one of the art and intelligence that conceived of the pavilion, while the Saul Leiter photo that accompanied it in the ill-fated but physically glorious Show *magazine is a most accurate photographic mirror of the Johnson we know.*

Robert A. M. Stern

Every little boy should have a tree house—every little girl a dollhouse. Every grown-up child should have his version of a playhouse, and this pavilion in a pond is mine.

If it be more than a little absurd to build playhouses today, will someone please tell me what is not absurd today?

My pavilion is full scale false scale, big enough to sit in, to have tea in, but really "right" only for four-foot-high people. Change of scale like this is a harmless and pleasant joke on serious architecture. And yet it is serious architecture, if architecture is to be defined as the art of making pleasant enclosures for people to be inside of. It is pleasant to be in a false scale—to feel big or feel small. How small you feel in St. Peter's false-scaled nave in Rome; how big in a doll's house. In my pavilion you feel big and important. When you sit for tea, you reduce yourself to child size and romantically enjoy the view through the seemingly countless arches, isolated from the world on a small island in a pond.

I designed and built the pavilion for two reasons: one, the place needed a gazebo and, secondly, I wanted deliberately to fly in the face of the "modern" tradition of functionalist architecture by tying on to an older, nobler tradition of garden architecture.

Both reasons gave me inordinate pleasure. In 1963, we are, I should imagine, thoroughly sick of Utilitarianism in all its forms, but one of the most banal effects of this philosophy has been its effect on the art of architecture. Usefulness as a criterion condemns our art to a mere technological scheme to cover ourselves from the weather, much as to say that shoes should be practical, not hurtful and handsome. Actually, there exist shoes designed just for comfort and we all know them for the hideously ugly monstrosities that they are. But somehow the idea has come about that mere functional (cheap) buildings are good enough for Americans. We no longer need beautiful buildings. But I say, just as in footwear, we need beautiful, in addition to mildly useful, buildings. My pavilion I should wish to be compared to high-style, high-heel evening slippers, preferably satin—a pleasure-giving object, designed for beauty and the enhancement of human, preferably blonde, beauty.

Fortunately, my place needed a gazebo badly. I had a pond—two years ago the place needed a pond—which looked rather empty. Something interesting to look at from the house was necessary. Contrariwise, some place to walk to from the house—from which to look at the house —was also necessary.

These "necessities" are, of course, meaningful only on the assumption that "gardens" constitute a vital part of the art of architecture. By "gardens," naturally, I do not mean places to grow flowers, but landscapes that have form and incident much as a great interior space must have form and incident. As a highboy gives emphasis to a gracious Colonial room, so a gazebo gives focus and meaning to an outside "room." "Gardens" in this sense are more important, bigger, more meaningful as works of architecture than even the greatest interior spaces.

Great ages have known this. Lenôtre in France and the English 18th-century Romantics all knew it. We are ignorant, but need we be, in an age—they tell us—of affluence? In any case, it is time someone started outdoor architecture on its way again. The William Morris—Walter Gropius cult of the useful must be overthrown. Grandeur we must reestablish.

My pavilion is too small to be grand I know, but the intent is there. If Louis (of any number) would give me the commission, or a Fouquet or a Burlington, what good big follies (*folies*) we could build! Follies in gardens—or arbors—or pavilions—or teahouses or summerhouses (as they were apologetically called in my Edwardian youth) must go on.

My moon-viewing pavilion (some still think of the Chinese tradition) is unusual for more than its peculiar scale. In the picture of the model you will see that there are four rooms placed around a small fountain. You will see canals which run in and out of the rooms—and an uncovered terrace. The rooms have names—for romantic association: the Entrance Hall, the Library, the Living Room, the Boudoir. It is the conceit that people in one room—all of eight-foot by eight-foot squares—cannot communicate with those in the adjoining one. Doors and walls are easily imagined. The tiny fountain is easily imagined, big and important.

The form of the design—the grammar—is frankly "modern." It seems useless to me to imitate past forms just because I wish to join a "noble" historical tradition. Forms always remain modern. The arcades are whimsical and most unclassically terminated; each interior corner, for example, holds up two different roofs at once. If the forms are modern, however, reminiscences abound: Moorish, Chinese, Palladian; traditions which are parents to all our design today.

The idea of the arch is, of course, contrary to "modern" design, the modern of the age of usefulness, because it is obvious these arches are not truly structural—not honest. But to me they are handsome and comforting. I use them often, at all sizes. The domes in my guest room are ten feet high as against the five-and-a-half of the pavilion. They have a calming, quieting effect on the guests—most enjoyable. The big 40-foot arches of the Sheldon Art Gallery in Lincoln, Nebraska, are monumental and should make the observer elated and give him heightened awareness for the fine arts within the building.

Arches big and small, carved or cast, with vaults or without, freestanding as in the pavilion, or engaged in the flat walls as in the Sheldon Art Gallery, are basically fascinating.

Arches on islands in a lake, doubly fascinating. Arches in full scale false scale, triply fascinating. Long live arches, long live follies.

Philip Johnson

From Perspecta, *9/10, 1965*

Whence and Whither:
The Processional Element in Architecture

Johnson's fundamental premise—that architecture can be qualified as any one thing, whether Wrightian-Rudolphian-Zevian "space," or Corbusian sculptural shapes (either mass or void), or his own "organization of procession"—seems uncharacteristically simplistic. Yet if one goes beyond this, the essay is a serious contribution to the as yet rather stunted body of modern architectural theory. Written especially for Perspecta, *it offers a clear analysis of the role of procession (i.e., spatial sequence in time) in archetypal situations, from the Parthenon through the Seagram Building and the Carpenter Center. Johnson reminds us that architecture is related to time, not in the pseudo-scientific way Giedion proposed, but in an experiential sense, dependent on the multiple perceptions of a man in motion and not frozen in place as in a photograph. In this regard, Johnson's essay can be seen as complementary to Christian Norberg-Schultz's writings and to the work of Kevin Lynch, especially his book* The Image of the City.

The false lure of photography is a theme Johnson returns to from time to time. Much as he admires the very cool, super-real photography of Ezra Stoller (he used to say that no building of his was "official" until it had been "Stollerized"), he, like his colleague, Henry-Russell Hitchcock, is critical of those who judge buildings from photographs, and, like Hitchcock, he almost never comments on a building he has not seen at firsthand, that is, experienced "processionally."

Robert A. M. Stern

Architecture is surely *not* the design of space, certainly not the massing or organizing of volumes. These are auxiliary to the main point, which is the organization of procession. Architecture exists only in *time*. (That is the modern perversion of photography. It freezes architecture to three dimensions, or some buildings to two.)

It is known to the veriest tourist how much more he enjoys the Parthenon because he has to walk up the Acropolis, how much less he enjoys Chartres Cathedral because he is unceremoniously dumped in front of it. How much better St. Peter's Square used to be before Mussolini ruined (opened up) the approaches. Vincent Scully's temples in *The Earth, The Temples and the Gods* are sited for approach as well as all the other considerations he has outlined for us.

But approach is only one aspect of processional, one moment of feeling. The next is the experience of entering, the shock of big space, or dark space, as it encloses (in time always) the visitor.

The Parthenon itself has no entering experience. Its entire feeling of procession is taken care of by the Propylaeum. The entire feeling of St. Peter's is taken care of, or was, by the filtering in through the barricade of Bernini's columns.

For modern examples take Mies's Seagram Plaza: the visitor crosses usually diagonally (an old Choisy-Beaux-Arts principle). Then he penetrates only glass, slowing slightly, to be faced with the three elevator corridors. But what elevator corridors! It seems simple enough, now that they are there, but compare these with any other. Where else in a modern skyscraper entry is the ceiling twenty-four feet high, or where else are the elevator lobbies in a direct line from the street? The visitor can look back to Park Avenue as he waits for the ride. In every other building there is a corner to be negotiated. The visitor has to wait in the first, second, or third box, has to take the first, second, or third turning to the left or right. In Seagram's it is a straight line.

Unfortunately, the entire experience of Seagram's leads but to the elevator, which, next to the automobile, ranks with the destroyers of architectural glory. That claustrophobic box brings visual, processional beauty to a complete dead stop. The visitor can only be restored, if at all, by looking out a high window. Elevators are here to stay, but one is not forced to love them.

Much better in that regard is the Guggenheim. (Never use the elevator! It murders Wright's great space.) The processional entrance experience is different from Mies's. It is again diagonal, but the jump into the hundred-foot-high hall is exactly the opposite kind of feeling from the typical grand axial entry to Seagram's. The visitor comes through a tiny door (too tiny, some feel) and is sprayed into the room. Breathtaking it is.

In both cases, the experiences are not static but temporal. The beauty consists in how you move into the space. There are as many ways of introducing space as there are architects, but it strikes me that clarity is one of the prerequisites. At least in the Guggenheim and in Seagram's the processional is as clean as the Acropolis or St. Peter's. The walker-through-the-space is never lost, ever in the slightest doubt as to his orientation, whence he has come or whither he aims. *Whence* and *whither* are positive, not negative, architectural virtues which are basic to the entire discipline of the art.

Take an extreme example, Le Corbusier's building for Harvard. Heaven knows it is easy to get lost in the basement. (What a surprise it is to come upon the "front" door with its label "Carpenter Hall.") Yet the building is, as a whole, a beautiful study in processional ex-

citement—even a study in "clarity." It is impossible to miss the effects that Le Corbusier has prepared. The shifting, rising, declining, turning path that he forces on us gives varied, solemn, laughable Coney Island experiences that please the stomach. The feeling of "entrance" is certainly lacking, since one enters only to be thrown out into the street in the next block, but what fun! (There is a report that the main entrances in the early studies used to be off the ramps. It would seem more logical than the present arrangement.)

In contrast, take Paul Rudolph's Art and Architecture Building at Yale (interestingly enough built to house similar functions to Le Corbusier's Harvard building). The approach is, to say the least, off axis. Like Frank Lloyd Wright's Buffalo Larkin Building, the main door does not exist. At Yale, bicycles are kept there. A postern entry only—a side gate. The explosion into space is again like Larkin and, like Larkin, very impressive indeed. These are, however, no further attempts at clarity, but rather a mannerist (do we dare use the word Mannerist?) play of spaces off the main space (Imperial Hotel Lobby?), which baffles and intrigues. I shall probably have to take back what I wrote in the previous page about clarity being of the essence. The House of Architecture has many mansions. There are, I guess, no rules.

But for me there are. So let us take an example from work in progress, my design for the temenos in which is to sit the Kline

Science Tower at Yale. Again the design may or may not succeed, but an artist's intention is at least of direct, though in the end only marginal, importance.

What I intend there is space seen in motion. A walk with change in direction with changing objectives. Also a slipping by of people, like a Giacometti "Place," like the diagonal walkings on the Seagram Plaza. Primary to this is clarity. One cannot, I hope, for a second be confused or, worse, annoyed in the turnings. One is forced to the entry of the Tower.

Walking up the hill at the upper end of Hillhouse, you enter through a propylaeum, a covered, columned portico. To the right the bastion of Gibbs; straight ahead—nothing. Perhaps in the future other buildings will rise above the cincture wall. Before you a paved square section with a colossal statue placed, I hope, inevitably; a point around which movement can circulate. Dominating your view is, however, immediately to your left, the Tower with its 100-foot-wide entrance steps. (It is too bad that the great increase in population has made great staircases obsolete. It was contrariwise lucky that the Mayans did not mind steep inclines. Our stair is modest.)

Before you enter the Tower, you note at the north, or right of it, a grove of young trees, shade, green in the summer, twigging in the winter.

An alien but relieving element. The temenos is not square but rectangular, and the Tower penetrates one corner far enough to call the remaining space an ell.

How it is enclosed is a major point. There can be no space without enclosure. West, a brick wall against Sterling (we are ten feet below grade here, which increases enclosedness), vines over the parapet, etc. The north, one brick wall, broken by an entrance from the Kline Chemistry on the left. The east corner, a vista—tightened by Gibbs and the wall—of East Rock, a visual proof that we are high ourselves. The east, Gibbs Laboratories; the south, the propylaeum and a retaining wall, a view down Hillhouse. A wall going down is as enclosing as one going up. Vézelay, Monte Pincio, Villa d'Este. And a going-down containment is a quiet eye relief from too much wall.

The processions through the plaza vary. There is a back stairs in the corner to the Tower. There is the entrance between Sterling and Osborn, one on the north corner, one at the north end of Gibbs, and Gibbs's front door itself. You should be able to get *from* any door *to* any door *clearly*. That is, at any rate, the intention. The means of clarification are porticos at all entrances; walks crossing the green are thin, uninterrupted visually one to the other.

Basically, the position of the Tower itself should clarify since it is strongly axial north and south. The Tower and the base of the Tower are *both* always visible. (It has always confused me that I still cannot find the bottom of that wholly admirable landmark, Harkness Tower. How many can remember what the ground floors of the Empire State Building look like from the street?)

Inside the building, whether you enter from the front or from the rear, you enter into the foyer facing the plaza, with the plaza on one side of the long hall, the elevators on the other. With the entering of the elevator, all processional is lost; it is the end of a chapter of architecture.

A few of the attempts and results of whither-whence: The New York State Theater, whatever stand one takes on its art works or decorative features, whatever one's views of Neo-classicism *vs.* concrete, is designed as a procession. The pop up the "baroque" stairs into the Mississippi-steamboat Promenade is of the essence. So are the side stairs up to and down from the upper balconies. So are the silhouetted moving people who form the living friezes to the space. This is all a question of procession.

Memory, by the way, plays a much larger part in architectural experience than is acknowledged. One feels better in a theater seat, I contend, if the spaces traversed getting there are uncrowded *straight*—in other words, clear.

Even a remodeling: the rearranged Museum of Modern Art is a case in point. The problem was to make possible bigger crowds than before. It was approached as a problem of procession. Confine the crowds as little as possible. The design result is almost Beaux-Arts axial. A clear main axial view into the garden from the street. A cross axis leading to galleries right and left. As usual, vertical flow stopped by elevators (only the elevators at the New York State Pavilion of the Fair are pleasant). In the garden we had more luck with the vertical. We took space enough for STAIRS in the old sense. We hope people will climb stairs, an experience lost in modern architecture, the ramps of the great Le Corbusier being the noble exception. In our garden about two domestic stories are climbed by many who would never go to the attic of a suburban house without complaining. It is the experience of the change of direction of what one sees as one rises. The speed of ascent (slow in the Museum stairs) is crucial. Time to look around, to feel the change that a rise gives. The curiosity of what is on top, the question: What will I see from up there? The comfort of a slow, obvious, and wide ascent. All of these considerations are more important than the "looks" of the stairway. Architecture is motion.

A final example, an old one. My own New Canaan house was started with the driveway. Such a disturbance is the automobile that its handling is the first consideration in the design of any home. In my house I had to buy the land next door to keep the monster from seeing my glass home. It now sits lurking behind a six-foot wall. The visitor gets out without seeing the house, rounds a corner (not 90°—

about 45°—very important) and sees the house at another 45°. Again a Choisy-Greek principle: never approach a building head on: the diagonal gives you a perspective of the depth of the building. To help you round the corner, to enhance the importance of the glass unit, there stands on the right a solid box, urging the visitor to turn away toward the Glass House.

The Glass House is on a promontory, a peninsula, to make a "cup" of the experience of entering. A dead end so you know you have arrived; there is no further to go. Within the house there is more procession, however. The "entrance hall" (the pushing together of the chimney and kitchen cabinet) forces you (gently, to be sure) between them into the "living room," where you climb onto the "raft" of white rug which is the ultimate arrival point, the sitting group which floats in its separate sea of dark brick.

I purposely exaggerate the processional aspects, which in reality are not obvious to the casual visitor. But then what is obvious to a visitor about the quality of architecture? I am supposed to be an architect, but I cannot tell you, nor can any historian, why the Parthenon is the masterpiece it is. We can but grasp bits and pieces.

The whence and whither is primary. Now almost secondary is all our ordinary work, our work on forms, our plans, our elevations. What we should do is to proceed on foot again and again through our imagined buildings. Then after months of approaching and re-approaching, and looking and turning, then only draw them up for the builder.

View of The Glass House, 1964.

Jacques Lipschitz sculpture, 1926-30, sits between the Brick Guest House, 1949, and, right, *The Glass House, 1949.*

View from the pond, winter 1975.

View of The Glass House with, right, *the Sculpture Gallery, 1982.*

Another view of interior looking west down the valley. Giacometti's "The Night," 1947, sits on a Mies van der Rohe table; "The Burial of Phocion" by Nicolas Poussin, 1648–49, is to right.

Interior of The Glass House with furniture by Mies van der Rohe.
Sculpture: "Two Circus Women" by Elie Nadelman, c. 1930, "Place"
by Giacometti, 1950 (right, on floor) *and "Conversation Piece" by*
Mary Callery, 1952 (center, on table).

View south from The Glass House to the Study, 1980.

A view of the entrance, 1952.

Clockwise: *Johnson leaning against the Guest House, 1950; Johnson in the hallway of the Guest House with Klee watercolors on wall, 1950; the bed and desk in The Glass House.*

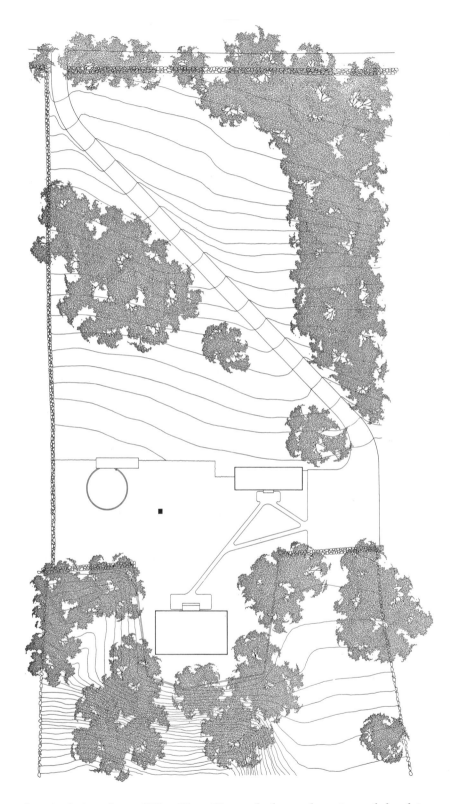

Original site plan of The Glass House before relocation of the drive-way, 1949.

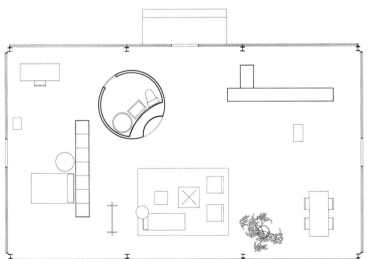

Top, *site plan of The Glass House (path to the pond,* at right, *was added later),* 1949. Bottom, *plan of The Glass House.*

Philip Johnson

From a lecture given at Columbia University, September 24, 1975

What Makes Me Tick

In the 1950's and early 1960's, Johnson was a frequent visitor at the leading architecture schools. He gave generously of his time as a visiting critic, a juror for studio projects, and a platform lecturer. While it would be convenient to say that the pace of his work in the office in the period after 1965 or the temporary decline of his energies in the early 1970's forced him to cut down on these activities, such would not be an honest account of the case. The reality of the matter is that in the unintelligible brutalizing of educational goals and standards which accompanied the, for me, rather more intelligible protests by university students and faculties over political situations at home and abroad in the time between Vietnam and Watergate, Johnson became persona non grata at most campuses. While architecture students mindlessly groped through a period of virulent anti-professionalism, of street-corner surveys, and courses in "how-to-build-your-own-yurt," Johnson came to be regarded as the enemy. All that articulate intelligence, cutting wit, and a much too substantial corpus of work alienated him from a generation of students who believed that those were precisely the most irrelevant attributes and achievements an architect could possess. Willing though the students of the late sixties were to sit for six, eight, nine befogged hours before a Buckminster Fuller, they would not offer even a quarter of an hour to Johnson, because they sensed in advance that Johnson knew about Fuller and knew about architecture, and could and would tell them about the differences between the two.

It is ironic and, for me, gratifying that Johnson's comeback to the university circuit was on the platform at Columbia in 1975. Johnson prepared his talk carefully, writing it down in advance, a most unusual thing for him to do. The message it imparts—the by-now eternal verities of his beliefs—is as clearly and convincingly stated as ever. One thing that is new and wonderful is the personal note, the willingness to talk about his own work not only in terms of the predictable list of predecessors and contemporaries, but also in terms of the younger generation.

After the miscalculations about the direction architecture was taking in the mid-1960's, as manifested in his review of Robin Boyd's book, Johnson began to look very carefully at the situation in design as it was emerging around him.

The work of the Venturis, Moore, and Giurgola began to interest him and provoke him to serious repose. The firm of Hardy/Holzman/Pfeiffer fascinates him, and he has written an unpublished essay about it; he admired Gwathmey enough to write an introduction to a book about his firm's work; and he also wrote a postscript to the second edition of the book Five Architects: Eisenman, Graves, Gwathmey, Hejduk, Meier. *He has been a faithful member of the audience at every occasion of importance when the work of young architects would be subjected to serious scrutiny. He knows the new scene very well, and while I don't think he likes all that much of what he sees—"likes," that is, in the sense that he is about to borrow from it—I do believe he can discuss it more intelligently than most.*

So we come almost to the present: Peck's Bad Boy is still bad; the rules are still there to be broken, the pretensions of architects to be stripped away, and the work of other architects freed of its protective camouflage of justifications and excuses and subjected to serious scrutiny. Only Johnson among our established architects can be counted on to provide this necessary criticism, and he can be counted on to do it for us because he cares so much for architecture. He continues to do it at this very writing and, one hopes, forever.

Robert A. M. Stern

What I would like to talk about today is what makes me tick; what goes through my mind when that awful moment comes in which I have to face the blank paper on the desk; what determines the direction of my thoughts; what makes the shapes of the buildings that come off the board.

I know what it used to be: the strict disciplines of the old International Style, a period I can look back on with less loathing, let me say, than you, or rather than Robert Venturi, the current brilliant guru of anti-modernism. I am nearly the last, Breuer and I perhaps, of the generation brought up on Le Corbusier-Bauhaus aesthetics, the aesthetics of the 1920's: Breuer as one of the young founders, myself as epigone.

We may not see a period like the twenties again for some time—the birth of a style of architecture built on commonly held beliefs in a few seemingly simple "truths." We really believed, in a quasi-religious sense, in the perfectibility of human nature, in the role of architecture as a weapon of social reform, in simplicity as a cure-all ("less is more"). We believed in expressing honestly the structure of a building, we believed with Laugier, Ruskin, Viollet-le-Duc, and Emerson in usefulness as an aesthetic criterion. Remember the early Museum of Modern Art exhibitions called "Useful Objects"? Not Beautiful Objects; Useful Objects. If something was useful, then a sort of halo descended upon it. The puritan ethic triumphed at last: only

simplicity was allowed—straight lines, narrow supports, cheap materials; only flat roofs, flat walls, and cubes were permissible. A style easier to describe with negatives.

There were, nonetheless, masterpieces. In spite of Le Corbusier's "*machine à habiter*," he built the Villa Savoye. In spite of Mies's "less is more," he built the Barcelona Pavilion. In spite of the fact that the word "Art" was forbidden at the Bauhaus, Gropius built the most artful Bauhaus building in Dessau.

But the beliefs of these leaders of fifty years ago sound quaint indeed today. I re-read with excruciating embarrassment a piece I wrote in 1931 defending our up-coming exhibition of architects at The Museum of Modern Art. (In those days "Modern" had a meaning.) Functionalistic clichés are laid end to end. Yet it was through those clichés that we hoped to sell what we really believed in: the coming utopia when everyone would live in cheap, prefabricated, flat-roofed, multiple dwellings—heaven-on-earth.

The utopia did not arrive. But beliefs are not related to actual results. And there have been many faiths in modern architecture. Besides the patent absurdity of *machines à habiter* and "less is more," recall Frank Lloyd Wright with "the horizontal line is the line of life" and Lou Kahn's "I ask the brick what it wants to be."

The day of ideology is thankfully over. Let us celebrate the death of the *idée fixe*.

There are no rules, only facts. There is no order, only preference. There are no imperatives, only choice; or, to use a nineteenth-century word, "taste"; or a modern word, "take": "What is your 'take' on this or that?"

Not that there are not some diehards. The Communists of the thirties have been succeeded by advocacy planners who still believe in salvation by architecture. There is the alternative culture whose members "do their thing" with faith in the results. There are technolators who believe with Bucky in salvation by the maximum of coverage with the minimum of materials, a Frei Otto who believes—and beautifully—in tension. There are some, mainly in England, who believe in the future of 4-by-8 panels that can be fitted by anybody, anywhere, for any purpose.

I can't honestly believe that all these are not a minority. I would like to hear from you on the subject provided that you want to be that articulate. (Parenthetically, there is no reason you should be articulate. Architecture is built with bricks and stones, not with words. But should you have beliefs, I would like to hear them.)

I am of the opinion that we have no faiths. I have none. "Free at last," I say to myself. However, shapes do not emerge from a vacuum. There are currents in the air. For example, historical architecture is "in" after almost a hundred years of neglect by the various "moderns" of the late nineteenth and twentieth century. True, we don't build in the Gothic style or the Re-naissance style, but we are not averse to inspiration at least. A Stirling with his dockyards, a Stern with his Lutyens, a Venturi with almost everybody, a Meier with his "take" on Corbu. So what—we cannot not know history.

Philosophically, it seems to me we today are anarchistic, nihilistic, solipsistic, certainly relativist, humorous, cynical, reminiscent of tradition, myth-and-symbol-minded rather than rationalistic or scientifically minded. What makes a building satisfactory—the word "beautiful" is more than ever treacherous—to Stern or Venturi, for instance, is bound to be different from what is satisfactory to me. *Vive la différence,* we live in a pluralistic society. So it is sometimes hard for me to understand what makes splendid architects like Chuck Moore or Aldo Giurgola (to pick at wide random) tick.

I can only talk about me. Maybe what makes me tick is unique. I don't mind, but it may be of interest to know how different my tick is from yours and yours.

Whenever I start a building design, three aspects—as I might call them—act as a sort of measure, aim, discipline, hope for my work.

First, the Aspect of the Footprint—that is, how space unfolds from the moment I catch a glimpse of a building until with my feet I have approached, entered, and arrived at my goal. In a church, the aspect of the footprint is simple; the hieratic procession to the altar itself. In a home, from the automobile the footprints may lead to a seat by the fire; in an office building, from the street to the elevator door. (The elevator, of course, being the death of processional architecture, my mind stops at its door.) The processional for most buildings, including homes, is complex, and in different eras is differently complex. At Ur in Mesopotamia five thousand years ago, the processional was also the architecture. Three enormous staircases that ascended eighty feet without landings, from three different directions, but all visible from the approaching visitor's path.

In Egypt it was a straight line, but what a straight line! very high, very low, wide, dense, straight to the holy of holies.

Most complex, on the Acropolis at Athens. You ascend on foot (the only tourist attraction that cannot be reached by auto, thank God) through the stark gateway. The colossal Athena Promachos on the right, near the back wall of the Pantheon, then the Erechtheum on the left, until in the full face of Mount Hymettos you make a 180° turn to face the unenterable Parthenon.

The medieval approach was a small diagonal street leading to a small square, where, facing nothing at all, usually off center in the piazza, stood the church. The bursting into the Piazza San Marco in Venice is a huge example.

The Baroque processional was symmetrical, straight, and grand; Versailles or St. Peter's, the grandest of all.

In modern times, at Taliesin West, Frank Lloyd Wright made the most intriguingly complex series of turns, twists, low tunnels, surprise views, framed landscapes, that human imagination could achieve.

In urban street and plaza design, we find the same differences of processional in different periods: the Greek, the interrupted gridiron street system, the medieval diagonal, the Baroque *allée*.

It is with this richness of processionals in mind that I try to imagine buildings.

Second, the Aspect of the Cave. All architecture is shelter; all great architecture is the design of space that contains, cuddles, exalts, or stimulates the persons in that space. It is the design of the cave part of a building that overrides all other design questions. Like Lao-tse's cup, it is the emptiness within that is of the essence.

There are lots of "insidenesses" to be studied besides the obvious interiors like Chartres Cathedral or the Grand Central Terminal. Nowicki once said all architecture is interior architecture—the Piazza San Marco in Venice, even the Acropolis in Athens, since walls that descend around you can hold you as securely as walls rising around you.

A plain box can hardly be an exciting cave; visit your local auto factory building. Nor does size alone count; once more visit your local auto factory. The modulation of interior space must have complexity: the side chapels of Brunelleschi's Santo Spirito, Michelangelo's transepts in St. Peter's, the spiral walks in the Guggenheim, the aisles of a hall church in the thirteenth century, the polychrome columns of Le Corbusier's

High Court in Chandigarh, the scale-shifting boulders floating in the Ryōanji Garden of Kyoto, are all tricks of molding caves to excite and thrill the observer. Spaces go in and out, up and down. They overlap, they cheat or suggest, all the time enriching the architectural experience. With all these noble paradigms in mind, I still like to try my hand at caves.

The third aspect, the most difficult, is the Building as a Work of Sculpture. Architecture is usually thought of as different from sculpture and indeed not much great architecture is sculpture, Pyramids, yes; Taliesin West, no. Stonehenge, perhaps; Versailles, no; the Guggenheim Museum, maybe. The Parthenon, certainly not. (Columns and entablatures see to that.) Frank Lloyd Wright roofs, arcades, colonnades, all speak architecture, not sculpture.

In the last few years, however, it seems to me sculptural forms, not necessarily geometric, have become a mark of architecture. As we have become impoverished in our external architecture by the lack of decorative motifs our forerunners could use—steeples, pointed and unpointed arches, and the like—we have turned to other modes of expression. Since there are no structural limitations today like the lintels of Stonehenge or the Parthenon, we can warp or carve or tilt our buildings the way we will. A wonderful example comes to mind: the fantastic gouges and the slithering angles of I. M. Pei's National Gallery addition—majestic, playful, abstract sculptures. Or take Kevin Roche's nine stelae at

Indianapolis (only three have been built): desert megaliths serving as an insurance company's headquarters.

These three aspects, the Footprint, the Cave, the Work of Sculpture, do not in themselves give form, but they are what I think about in the night away from the boards, when I try to brush away the cobwebs of infinite possibilities and try to establish some way out. Very frustrating.

By no accident, the best illustration from my own work of the three aspects is a building I built for my own delectation in 1970 in New Canaan: the Sculpture Gallery, which many of you have seen, at least in magazines. First, the Footprints. Here the exterior approach is straight down a three-hundred-foot *allée* of maples. No diagonal, no steps, no space warp. The interior, on the other hand, is a play of changing directions.

The main entrance, the "gozinta" I call it, is the key to any building. What is your first impact? How does it prepare you for the future experience? Do you stop in wonder? Do you perhaps enter in a low tunnel as at Taliesin West to burst into a great space? The "gozinta" here is a glass door giving a glimpse of a room of Don Judd sculptures to the right. The left is cut off by a wood partition above eye height, which gives you a six-foot space to reveal to you the glass roof, the white walls, but conceals the surprise view down to the main pentagonal space twelve feet below. The way then proceeds along a parapet (twelve inches high to create tension and fear), a right angle to the left. The room (the building is only one room; Mendelsohn was right—an architect is remembered for his one-room buildings) changes radically a few steps further with Robert Morris's sculpture at the right. Seven steps down, then a 45° turn, seven more steps, a new view of the room. You are now on a bridge—below to the left, still the focal space below; on the right, the Flavin sculpture room. A 90° turn and seven more steps, and you have curled around the focal space and landed at the bottom. You carom off the entrance wall and settle down a turn and a quarter from the entrance door like a dog which has sniffed out a room and settles circularly into his place.

The gallery also illustrates the second aspect, the Aspect of the Cave. Although it is one room, the four peripheral bays facing four of the five sides of the central area each form three-sided rooms, the fourth side opening on and enlarging the main space, like open-sided chapels of a church. The glass roof covers all four of these bays as well as the focal space, sheltering the entire complex. You sit or stand in this focal space, the stairs slicing and around you, but beyond and above you stretch the four bays on the four sides of a pentagonal focal space, the fifth side being the entrance wall. The space is broken into sub-spaces. All of its three thousand square feet are visually usable, though each of the five sub-spaces is intimate within its own perimeter. This doubling of the spaces, or rather the borrowing and overlapping of the four side

bays with the focal space, is what I was trying to learn from Frank Lloyd Wright's great lobby of the Imperial Hotel in Tokyo.

Let us now talk of the third aspect—Sculpture. On the outside the building has the shape of a southern Spanish white barn gone awry. The ridge beam is set diagonally to the main rectangle, suggesting many 45° and 135° angles jarringly juxtaposed.

The most successful sculpture that John Burgee and I have built is Pennzoil Place in Houston. Two trapezoidal buildings each composed, if you can imagine it, of a square plus a right triangle, that almost meet at a point in their corners, each roof sloping 45° toward each other. In plan, each building of course has a 45° point at the triangle. The ridges of the buildings, however, are also broken to slope away to a corner, giving the rather absurd impression of a twisted parrot's beak. At the base there are two courts, again with roofs that pitch 45° up a hundred feet high, tapering in plan to ten feet wide.

The work of sculpture sounds more complex than it is. Straight walls, or 45° slanted walls; no roof at all. The plan is orthogonal, with occasional 45° elements. All is play of simple angular volumes. But these simple volumes meet at the all-important ten-foot slot which is the key of the design—a non-volume which makes the sculpture. The gap is visible, but only sometimes; the rest of the time it is a mystery known about, but unseen. Parenthetically, it must be admitted that the processional element of Pennzoil is really automobilistic. The parrot's beaks, the surprising slot, are best seen from the freeways that surround the city.

Another building of John Burgee and mine which illustrates the processional and cave aspects of our work is the I.D.S. complex in Minneapolis. The Crystal Court there has become the "living room" of the city. The crowds are huge. They come to buy Baskin-Robbins ice-cream cones and to watch the girls—and our balconies and our processional make it easy, inevitable, for them to enjoy the experience.

Luck we certainly had. Bridges on all four sides bring in more people than the four entrances on the street level. Minneapolitans are trained by their Siberian climate to bridge their streets to keep warm. So we had our two-level city to start with—a dream situation for an architect. To help our luck, however, we were very careful about our "gozintas." On each of the four sides, a zigzag funnel pierces the façades, narrowing often twenty or thirty feet to an eighteen-foot wide entrance. The visitor then bursts after a short tunnel into the Crystal Court: a room covered with clusters of glass cubes that pile asymmetrically to a hundred-foot-high apex. Again asymmetrically placed against a diagonal

wall, we placed a high-speed escalator to the balconies, which wind their way around the Court and lead in turn out over the lower funnels to four buildings across the streets.

Thus, we like to think, the eight entrances to the cave, the enforced diagonal of the balcony, the clarity of four entrances, four compass points, make pleasant processions. We like to think that the design of our cave, mounting to a crazy high point, decorated with the balcony ribbon and its slanted escalator and its peculiar pentagonal shape, with no two sides the same length, making an odd centrality with its surrounding walls constantly zigging and zagging in 5-by-10-foot orthogonal modules creating a basic rhythm, helps the excitement that all people seem to feel in the room.

John Burgee and I have had fun the last few years with shapes and funnels, plazas, "gozintas," indoor streets, sloped sides and/or roofs, making processionals, spaces and sculptures. We have even finished a 1930's ribbon-window, round-cornered, setback building in Houston. What a grand period for us to live in today!

Contrariwise, what will all this sound like in ten years?

View, opposite, *of the House at night, 1949.*

Robert Hughes

From Time, *October 26, 1970*

The Duke of Xanadu at Home

It is 7:30 of a fall Sunday evening and only a few artists remain, straggling under spotlighted trees across the shaven lawns of Philip Johnson's 32-acre New Canaan precinct. All the millionaires and collectors have gone home. Andy Warhol, in black jacket and silver wig, looking like the Angel of Death quitting Jerusalem, left ten minutes ago. Robert Rauschenberg lingers on, and though a lady art critic is locked in Johnson's subterranean painting gallery with a young artist who is slapping her around for undetermined reasons, the place is quiet. Above the Morrises, Judds and Oldenburgs, lights still burn in the new sculpture gallery, the completion of which was the occasion for the party. Through the glass wall of his house, a few hundred feet away, the host watches the Connecticut sky display its sense of occasion by turning a fulgid, Turneresque pink. Philip Johnson, architect and art collector, scans his horizon with pleasure as if the sunset, too, were a commissioned work. The inauguration of his own special Xanadu is nearly over.

Up from the Top. Johnson's sculpture gallery, with its complex flows of space and rafter-striped light, is a far cry from his 1949 Glass House, but it may, in time, become as famous. Between them lies a career of almost indecent success, starting near the top: wealthy by inheritance, Johnson is now, at 64, one of the three or four best-known architects alive in America.

There is no "school" of Johnson, as there was of his own great mentor, Mies van der Rohe, with whom he worked on the design of New York's Seagram Building. Indeed, it is hard to imagine a young architect setting out to imitate Johnson. He is an architect of sensibility, not polemics, and his work has no discernible core of aesthetic theory. It is all taste, exemplary in its detailing and finesse of decision. Though he was trained in the strict, functionalist idiom of Mies and Gropius, Johnson believes such purism "is winding up its days." "Structural honesty," he declared in 1961, "seems to me one of the great bugaboos that we should free ourselves from very quickly."

Dolphin in History. Johnson does not see buildings simply as machines for living. For him, the need for fantasy, play, memory and spectacle is just as real as the need for efficiency. Most of all, in Johnson's view, people need a sense of history. Architecture cannot give it to them by making ebullient panty raids on the sleeping past, grabbing a cornice here, a vault or pilaster there. It is a matter of integration. Not many architects now living have Johnson's integrative powers. He is a highly educated architect, able to slip like a dolphin through the currents of style: history is his natural element, and from the last 20 years of Johnson's output it is clear that he took to a manner of free-wheeling historical allusion as his proposed alternative to the International Style—which by 1950 had frozen from a mainstream into a glacier, trapping its architects in ice like mastodons.

Perhaps Johnson's most revealing work is what he put up for Johnson—his enclave in New Canaan, built over a span of 21 years and now completed by the sculpture gallery. Johnson dislikes calling it an estate, preferring the word compound— but an estate it is, with all the seigneurial overtones. There has, in fact, been nothing like it since the ducal properties of 18th century England.

Theatrics of Neatness. Who else has a switch on his terrace that, at the flick of a whim, causes a fountain to spurt 120 feet into the air from the center of a private lake? Johnson's house is a monument to the theatrics of neatness: only a bachelor could sustain such stark elegance at this pitch of obsession—one three-year-old child could reduce it all to chaos in ten minutes. It is perhaps the expression of a dilettante—in the classic sense of the word, a lover of the fine arts. It does need money, but it also demands concern. Johnson noted that the trunks of oaks turn dark after rain while maples stay light; he has judiciously pruned the forest surrounding his house to produce the most satisfactory chiaroscuro possible after every passing storm.

But if Johnson indulges himself in the dilettante pleasures, he scorns the corresponding idleness. He has designed ten art galleries, and his work in Manhattan includes the New York State Theater, the extensions to the Museum of Modern Art, Asia House and the library for New York University. An unceasing flow of projects issues from his office in the Seagram Building, and currently he shares with Paul Rudolph and Kevin Roche an exhibition at the Museum of Modern Art called "Work in Progress." It includes models of Johnson's glass arcades for N.Y.U. modeled on the Milan Galleria but as high as Beauvais Cathedral; a tumbling water garden for Fort Worth; slanted prismatic skyscrapers for Minneapolis.

Dwarfs and the Duke. An art historian can read Johnson's development simply by studying the buildings on the estate—Johnson himself admits that here he tries out his ideas. "I have never felt free working for a client," he acknowledges. "But working for oneself is a different matter. You have to discover your own needs. That is not easy, but it leaves you free."

The first building was Johnson's own house, the idea for which—a house built entirely of glass—Mies van der Rohe proposed to him in 1946. A transparent box with one opaque brick cylinder than contains the bathroom, the house has since become a classic of American architecture, and even after 21 years it is a startlingly expressive building—not least for the intelligence and openness with which it states its prototypes. The "absolute" cubic form was taken from one of the 18th century fathers of modern architecture, Claude Ledoux. Le Corbusier provided the angling paths between the transparent, almost invisible house and the solid brick guesthouse (each building becomes the positive-negative image of the other). And so on. Johnson took his idea for the lake pavilion—a caprice of scale, with concrete colonnades only six feet high and three feet wide—from the miniaturized dwarfs' quarters in the Renaissance ducal palace in

Mantua. "Obviously the duke didn't build them that way to make the dwarfs happier. It made *him* feel happier." In 1965, Johnson added the subterranean gallery for his paintings. It was modeled—perhaps appropriately, considering the value of the Stellas, Rauschenbergs and Warhols that hang there—on the ancient Treasury of Atreus in Mycenae. The paintings are hung on huge leaflike screens, which swing like the pages of a book, a means of display Johnson adapted from the Soane Museum in London.

Shifting Light. Johnson's new sculpture gallery is a brilliant attack on the problem of how to avoid a long, boring, enfiladed room of sculpture without chopping the space up into unrelated cubicles. Johnson's deceptively complex plan ("I wanted to see what could be done with 45-degree angles; we all know about right angles") places the sculpture in related groups on different levels around a central, five-sided well; the inflections of this space, its arrest and flow, are masterly. The gallery is flooded with shifting light from the roof, which consists of tubular steel rafters supporting narrow panes of mirror glass that both reflect the sculptures and transmit the dazzling blue of the sky. The ambiguity of space, and its constant surprises, allows each sculpture to make its own zone of authority. It may be that in this building Philip Johnson has done for the pseudo religion of art what Corbusier, in his chapel at Ronchamp, did for the modern church.

Paul Goldberger

From Smithsonian Magazine, *September 1975 (Volume 5, Number 11)*

From Philip Johnson's Eminent, Elegant, Practical World

There are few architects who could claim, as Philip Johnson can, that they live, work and weekend in buildings which they designed themselves. But Johnson spends his weekday nights in a townhouse on East 52nd Street in New York which he designed in 1952, goes to work in the Seagram Building on Park Avenue, which he designed in association with Mies van der Rohe in 1958, and escapes each weekend to his famous glass house of 1949 in New Canaan, Connecticut.

Johnson's situation is made more curious still by the fact that all three buildings derive from the early, or "Miesian" period in his career, when he was perhaps the late architect's chief propagandist (he published a book on Mies' work in 1947) and all of his own work was rather unashamedly Mies-inspired. Now Johnson's work is markedly different: After a middle period

of somewhat overdelicate classicism (an obvious, and sometimes rather strained, attempt to break free from the grip of Mies' austere steel-and-glass vocabulary), he has moved on to do a series of buildings which are notable for a freshness of form which confirms his position as one of the most inventive designers in America today.

Johnson's career as an architect has been marked by a rejection of rules and theories; he is too fascinated by pure form for that. Yet his work is saved from the superficiality of change for its own sake by a superbly disciplined design intelligence which demands an intellectual justification for every new form, and sees every building as part of a larger problem of architectural history. Vincent Scully, the architectural historian, put it best when he called Johnson "admirably lucid, unsentimental, and abstract, with the most ruthlessly aristocratic, highly studied taste of anyone practicing in America today. All that a nervous sensibility, lively intelligence, and a stored mind can do, he does."

Johnson, a scholar by training who came into architecture after years as an architectural historian, has always been one of the few architects in this country to acknowledge freely the importance of history in contemporary design; the "stored mind" to which Scully refers was admitting the validity of historical allusions while many other modernists were still indulging in the Bauhaus fantasy of breaking clear of historical precedent. For Johnson, then, his own Miesian buildings are now themselves history—he works in the Seagram Building as he might work in Louis Sullivan's Wainwright Building, as a place to be learned from but no longer to be imitated. And so it is, too, with the 52nd Street house and the glass house.

The glass house, 25 years old, is the building which architects and non-architects alike associate with Johnson most quickly, and it remains not only an extraordinary building in itself but as effective a key to his way of thinking about and making architecture as it was when it was built.

Like all of the great houses architects have designed for themselves, Johnson's building in New Canaan had a function far more subtle than that of a proving ground for new ideas. Instead of trying to produce something altogether new (which it was),

Johnson took the Miesian approach and continually refined it, not broadening but narrowing the scope until he had what he could consider a perfect object.

The result was a glass box, 56 feet long, with furniture groupings defining the use areas. There are no partitions; only a round brick cylinder containing a bathroom rises to the ceiling.

From inside, the carefully manicured landscape visible through the glass functions as an enclosure, and the ironic illusion is superb: The vistas tell the occupant he is open to the whole world, while in truth there is no world outside at all—just an elegantly arranged landscape that is as much a part of the house as the furniture. The "real world" toward which the walls of glass beckon is far away and invisible.

Since the glass house was completed, it has grown into a compound of five buildings, and if the house itself is a relic from an earlier era, the overall grouping reflects all of the phases of Johnson's career. The guesthouse, all of brick, is in deliberate counterpoint to the glass house. (Just recently Ellsworth Kelly's *Quarter Arc,* a huge sculpture of rusted steel which is the latest addition to Johnson's impressive collection of contemporary art, was installed nearby, its form itself in counterpoint to the guesthouse.) The lush interior of the guesthouse reflects Johnson's first post-Miesian phase, as does the small, elegant white-columned pavilion by the lake, its unexpectedly small size playing the sort of trick of scale which fascinates and delights Johnson.

Two more recent buildings complete Johnson's estate: his art gallery of 1965 and sculpture gallery of 1970, each of which symbolizes yet another direction. The art gallery is an "underground" building, set into a hill above the glass house. Pictures from Johnson's extensive collection of contemporary art are displayed on panels hung around three circular areas which together make up the gallery space. The panels can be adjusted to change the pictures on display at any one time and, in doing so, redefine the entire room. If the glass house eliminated traditional walls, it at least implied them in the ironic tension it set up between inside and outside; in the art gallery the moving walls constitute what is actually a more radical expression.

The sculpture gallery is a sharply defined, irregular white structure, a sort of angular Guggenheim Museum, with levels stepping downward around a central space, the whole room marvelously tense, all covered with a greenhouselike glass roof.

Taken together, the buildings on his estate at New Canaan are a remarkable group; far more than the ultimate expression of one man's personal taste, they represent an attempt to come to grips, over time, with a variety of notions of what architecture is. They are the result of an agile mind probing, refining, rethinking, from the glass house's explorations within the Miesian vocabulary and ironic interplay of inside and outside, to the art and sculpture galleries' newer, more striking forms and uses of space.

Johnson once delighted in showing guests through the compound, not only to show it off but as an excuse to converse about architecture—which, in spite of the frequency with which he is seen at all sorts of New York gatherings, is the only subject he ever really *wants* to talk about. Now, at age 68, he prefers to spend his weekends more quietly and limits most visits to old friends—although he did open the house and grounds to 225 members of the Architectural League of New York, who came to celebrate the 25th birthday of the glass house.

Calvin Tomkins

From The New Yorker, *May 23, 1977*

From **Forms Under Light**

From the beginning of his career, Philip Johnson's best client has always been Philip Johnson, and his best-known work is still the glass house that he built for himself in 1949, on a green hillside in New Canaan. Just about every architecture critic has either praised it or condemned it, and in 1950 *The Architectural Review* of London, the profession's leading international journal, devoted eight pages to it. In the article, Johnson himself, breaking all precedent, discussed the historical and contemporary sources of his design. These included Le Corbusier, Theo van Doesburg, the Acropolis, Karl Friedrich Schinkel, Claude Nicholas Ledoux, Kazimir Malevich, and most particularly, Mies van der Rohe, who as early as 1945 had discussed with Johnson his concept of a house built entirely of large sheets of glass. Mies, in

fact, had designed a glass house for Dr. Edith Farnsworth in Plano, Illinois, and Johnson had seen the plans for this house, whose completion was delayed until 1950. Johnson has never made the slightest effort to conceal his debt to Mies or his use of specific details from the Farnsworth house. The two houses are very different, though, and the differences are revealing. The Farnsworth house is a floating glass rectangle, narrower than Johnson's, raised on metal columns above the floodplain of the Fox River (raised not quite high enough, it turns out; the water occasionally comes in) and sandwiched between two horizontal planes of white-painted steel. Johnson's house rests on the ground, on the shelf of a hill, and its steel frame is painted black. The Farnsworth house is a sculptural object in a landscape; Johnson's is part of the landscape, a semitransparent image that sometimes reflects its surroundings and sometimes seems to disappear as you look at it. "It doesn't have as good details as the Farnsworth," Johnson has said. "It hasn't got the absolute refinement, the pure white, floating elegance of that rather cold masterpiece." Most people who have seen both consider Johnson's house infinitely the more hospitable, and it has certainly had more influence on architectural history. "I think it's one of the most important buildings in America," the Yale art historian Vincent Scully said last spring. "The glass house is a real archetype—a fundamental piece of architecture, like a life-support pod—and as such it is full of suggestions for the future."

A Sunday in spring—warm but not hot, with a slight breeze stirring the leaves of the big oaks that shade the glass house, where Philip Johnson and some friends and I are enjoying a late lunch. In palmier times, in the early sixties, Johnson had a staff of servants and entertained lavishly—up to fourteen for lunch nearly every weekend, and sometimes for dinner as well. (The servants lived in a conventional house on the property, which Johnson bought when he discovered that his glass house offered none of the more prosaic amenities, such as storage space.) Now he lives more simply. He uses his weekends at the glass house mainly to read and to work. This is where he does most of his designing.

"One problem with glass houses is when an inside wall hits the glass," Johnson says. "If that happens, you don't have a glass house anymore. How do you provide rooms and yet never touch the glass with a partition?" Both Johnson and Mies solved it by having no partitions. The bathroom, fireplace, and service facilities in Johnson's house are contained in a circular, freestanding brick cylinder that breaks through the flat roof like a big chimney, and that appears from the outside to anchor the house to its site. (In the Farnsworth house, the service core does not extend through the roof line.) The bathroom unit divides the "bedroom," at the far end of the house, from the "living room," an austere arrangement of Mies van der Rohe stainless-steel-and-brown-leather furniture on a white rug. The dining table and chairs (also Mies) are at the near end, opposite a waist-high kitchen unit. There are only two works of art: a sculpture of two women by Elie Nadelman, near the kitchen unit, and "The Death of Phocion," painted by Nicolas Poussin and acquired by Johnson in 1946 (his only noncontemporary work of art), on an easel near the fireplace. Johnson's friend Rosamond Russell (formerly Rosamond Bernier) remembers coming here for the first time, in the nineteen-sixties, with the Barrs and casually dropping her handbag on the Mies chaise longue. Marga Barr quickly corrected her, whispering that one does not leave extraneous objects lying about in the glass house. The interior is a still-life.

Another problem with glass houses is the practical one of privacy. Johnson's solution to this was landscaping. His house overlooks a valley, also owned by him, that has been cleared of all but the largest trees; in the valley are a man-made pond, inhabited by two Canada geese and a school of venerable goldfish, and a little white pavilion—a concrete "folly." Though its myriad arches and columns are only half the normal scale, and one can enter it only by ducking one's head, it looks full-scale from the glass house. (The pond used to have a water jet that rose to a height of a hundred and twenty feet, but no longer; it was too expensive to operate, and the pump has been removed.) Because the glass house was built in the middle of a hill rather than on top of one, its uphill side could be screened from the road by a high stone wall and by trees and other plantings, and also by a solid brick guesthouse, which was completed in 1949, shortly before the glass house, and which is, in a sense, its antithesis—an opaque rectangle with three porthole-type windows. Over the years, Johnson has bought up land on either side of his property, so that the original five acres have increased to thirty-two. His privacy is well established, although, as the architecture critic Paul Goldberger once observed, in order to live successfully in Philip Johnson's glass house one would probably have to be Philip Johnson.

After lunch, Johnson and I walked down to the little pavilion, following a zigzag path through woods carefully pruned of everything but wild flowers. (Johnson still employs a gardener.) "This was my most extreme break with the Miesian aesthetic and the International Style," Johnson said of the pavilion. "I built it in 1962, mainly to thumb my nose at modern architecture that had to have a use." Having been responsible in large part for establishing the International Style in this country, Johnson was one of the first to abandon it. His pavilion is an exercise in sheer, history-laden playfulness, and as such it has outraged every true-blue modernist. "I was thinking about the quarters that the Duke of Mantua made for his dwarfs, in the sixteenth century," Johnson said as we sat down on the concrete floor. (When we were sitting down, our heads were at the level they would have been in a normal room if we had been standing up.) "Also about an island house, like the one you see in Böcklin's 'Island of the Dead.' Also about tree houses and doll houses—the appeal of the small. At that time, I was working on the Mondrian plan—you can see how this is all built on squares, differently treated. And I was also working on the basic problem of the Renaissance, which was how you turn corners in a columnar system—you see, I've invented a column here that turns all ways, inside and out, without any change of pattern, which was something they never did in the Renaissance. And one more thing I had in mind was the great Moslem mosque in Córdoba, with all those columns that you look through, and with that sense of mystery. I even put gold leaf on the ceiling, you see. It's disintegrating now, but it makes a wonderful contrast with the concrete. When I had servants, I'd put down straw mats and we'd have little *fêtes champêtres* in here—all sorts of Pompeian conceits."

. . .

"What did Mies think about your glass house?" I asked, a bit later.

"He never said anything to me about it, one way or another," Johnson replied. "But I know that his students in Chicago always considered it a poor imitation of his Farnsworth house, so that's probably what he thought. He came here many times, but then one night we got into a philosophical argument about something, and Mies became so angry that he insisted on spending the night under another roof. I had to drive him to a neighbor's. The next day he apologized, and our relationship continued, but he never again set foot in the house. Frank Lloyd Wright was much more outspoken, of course. He hated the whole International Style, which he called 'flat-chested.' Wright really built the Edgar Kaufmann house, Fallingwater, as an answer to our 1932 show at the museum—as though he were saying, 'All right, if you want a flat roof, I'll show you how to really build a flat roof.' It was a wonderful answer. But that was in 1938, and we didn't know then how good Wright was. I thought he was good but terribly old-fashioned. Russell

Hitchcock and I went to see him at Taliesin, in Wisconsin, when we were planning the 1932 show. He had no phone, and there were two-by-fours under all the cantilevers, and the plumbing didn't work. He'd hardly built anything in ten years. But he was just as determined as ever. What appealed to him about Russell and me was that we were really interested in the art of architecture. I remember one time Wright came into my glass house and stood there, wearing one of his wide-brimmed hats, and said, 'Philip, should I take my hat off or leave it on? Am I indoors or am I out?' Then, in the fifties, I made the mistake of referring to him in a lecture as 'the greatest architect of the nineteenth century,' and he heard about it and was furious. The next time we saw each other was at Yale. He came up to me and said, 'Why, Philip, I thought you were dead.' And later he said, 'Little Phil, all grown up and building houses and leaving them out in the rain.'" (Vincent Scully, who was present, remembers that Wright was so pleased with himself over this sally that he became positively benign for the rest of the evening.) "Wright joked about my house, but he kept coming back," Johnson said. "His eyes stayed open."

. . .

In place of history, Johnson looked to contemporary American art for inspiration. Although he had been buying paintings for years, he did not really start to collect in earnest until the sixties, and what he collected then was Pop and Minimal art. Advised by his friend David Whitney, who is a museum consultant, he bought early works by Robert Rauschenberg and Jasper Johns, the artists who led the way out of Abstract Expressionism, and shortly thereafter he began buying Andy Warhol, Roy Lichtenstein, and Frank Stella. In 1965, he built his own paintings gallery on the New Canaan estate, burying it in the hillside so that it would not interfere with the view of or from the glass house. Johnson also collected the spare, reductionist "primary structures" of the Minimal sculptors Donald Judd, Dan Flavin, and Richard Serra, as well as the antiformal soft sculptures of Robert Morris and Claes Oldenburg, and in 1970 he completed a sculpture gallery on his estate to house them. All these young artists were thumbing their noses at tradition (this naturally appealed to Johnson), and most of them had dispensed more or less completely with the technical skills—the fine craftsmanship—that used to be considered an essential component of painting and sculpture. The Pop artists' celebration of the ordinary and the banal— of beer cans and advertising art and comic-strip images—carried over into architecture mainly through the work of the Venturis (Robert Venturi and his wife, Denise Scott Brown), who saw Las Vegas and the suburban shopping strip as legitimate architectural models for our time.

Johnson himself was more directly influenced by the geometric simplifications of Minimal sculpture—in his John F. Kennedy Memorial, in Dallas, for instance, and his Art Museum of South Texas, in Corpus Christi. The austerity and the unadorned, direct quality of these recent works have obvious affinities with his earlier, Miesian buildings, but the spirit is different— cruder, stronger, more closely related to the surrounding environment. The spirit, in fact, is wholly contemporary.

. . .

The tour of the New Canaan estate usually ends in the sculpture gallery. It is near the northern boundary of the property—a low-lying structure that fits into the hillside as comfortably as the line of maples that mark what must once, a hundred years ago or more, have been a farm road. The exterior walls are white-painted brick. The roof is glass—the same sort of mirrored glass that Johnson used later in the lobby of Pennzoil Place in Houston, and will use throughout the Crystal Cathedral in Garden Grove. Inside, the tubular-steel framework of the roof casts a grid of barred shadows on the white brick walls—an unplanned effect that is very pleasing. (There is a certain element of luck in architecture; Johnson did not know when he designed the metal chain-link curtains for the windows of the Four Seasons restaurant that they would be in continuous, rippling motion.) The gallery itself is one large room on five levels, with a twisting stairway down the center. Each landing becomes, in effect, a separate room, yet all of them can be seen from any other. (Only a sixth space, at the very bottom, is not visible from the top.) The lines here are all diagonals and forty-five-degree angles. It looks immensely complicated architecturally, but Johnson says it is very simple—"two almost-cubes that have been partially twisted." The sculptures are wonderfully visible in the soft natural light—big pieces, mostly, by Mark di Suvero, Donald Judd, Bruce Nauman, Robert Rauschenberg, and others. "It's perfect nondirectional light," Johnson explains. "Only fourteen per cent of the light comes through the mirrored glass, which makes it cool, and you can keep your eyes open just as though you were in the shade. This is where I work now on weekends; it's a perfect concentrational place. To me, it's still the best room I've ever done. The best way to see it is with people around—they make the decoration."

Map

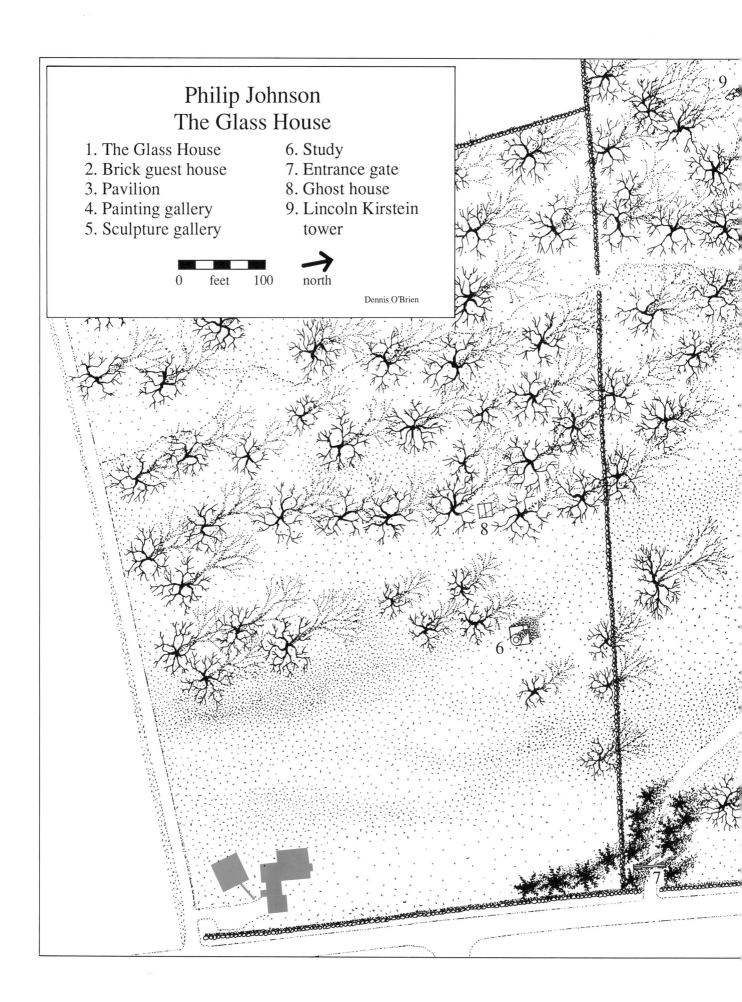

Philip Johnson
The Glass House

1. The Glass House
2. Brick guest house
3. Pavilion
4. Painting gallery
5. Sculpture gallery
6. Study
7. Entrance gate
8. Ghost house
9. Lincoln Kirstein tower

0   feet   100   north

Dennis O'Brien

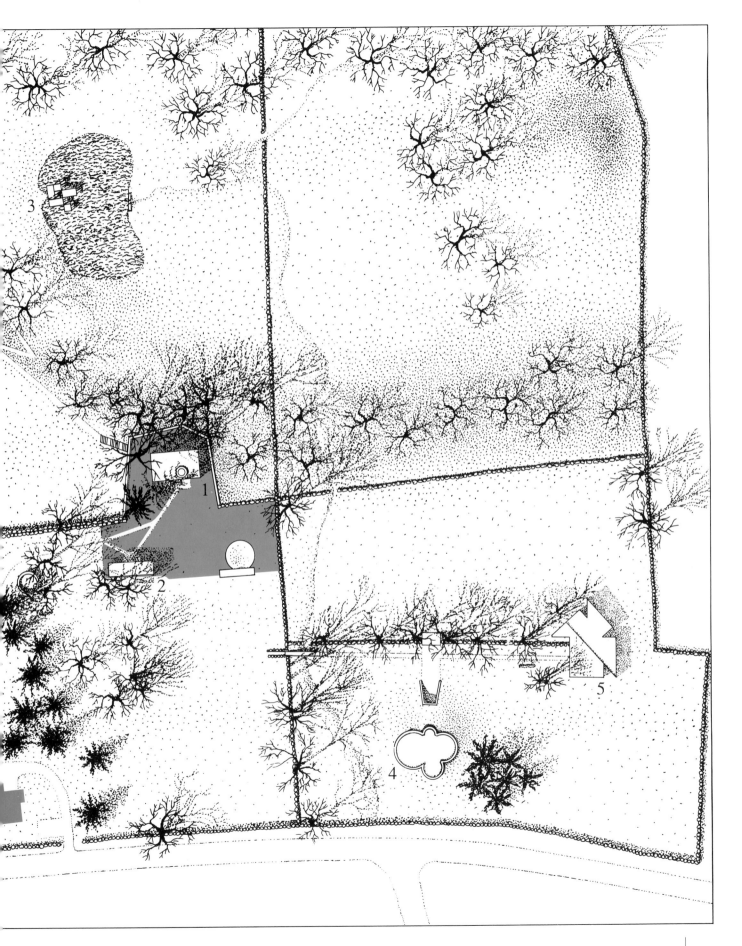

Robert A. M. Stern

From Oppositions, *Fall 1977*

The Evolution of Philip Johnson's Glass House, 1947–1948[1]

In an article in the *Architectural Review* written in 1950 Johnson outlined his views on the relationships between the compositional principles seen in his work at New Canaan and various historical examples.[2] In that same article he acknowledged his indebtedness to Mies van der Rohe for the very idea of the Glass House: "Mies had mentioned to me as early as 1945 how easy it would be to build a house entirely of large sheets of glass. I was skeptical at the time, and it was not until I had seen the sketches of the Farnsworth House that I started the three-year work of designing my Glass House. My debt is therefore clear, in spite of obvious differences in composition and relation to the ground."[3]

Despite this assertion of skepticism by Johnson, the assumption generally held has been that the final design was chiefly an outgrowth of Johnson's unquestioning admiration for Mies. It supposedly followed a logical progression from Johnson's own earlier Ash Street House in Cambridge of 1942 by way of his first house built for a client, the Eugene Farney House of 1947, and was crystallized by his viewing of Mies's early drawings for the Farnsworth House. Now, with the publication of these early studies, the story of the Glass House can be seen to be much more complex if less romantic. For these early studies shatter the image of Johnson as a confirmed Miesian who mined the master's best ideas only to turn away from his example in mid-career in search of a more personal style. They suggest a very different Johnson, from the very beginning of his career, different from both the early polemicist for the International Style and the admirer and disciple of Mies, and one already strongly involved in a renascent form of German Romantic Classicism.

Though most of the drawings for the Glass House are Miesian in vocabulary, there are important exceptions, most notably the "Syrian arch" scheme, which appears late in the chronological sequence. It not only seems as well developed as any other of the studies but it is also as literal in its historical eclecticism as any work of Johnson's in his so-called ballet school phase of the late 1950's and early 1960's. The scheme—really an essay in German Romantic Classicism inspired by Schinkel and Persius—encourages one to speculate on what might have been built in New Canaan had Johnson not been working closely with Mies in 1946–1947 on the preparation of the exhibition of Mies's work at The Museum of Modern Art and thus having seen the early drawings for the Farnsworth House. It also raises the issue of historical eclecticism in Johnson's work almost a decade before it emerged in the work of other architects of the Modern Movement. Is this issue to be interpreted as a precursor of a more general condition or is it merely an eccentric manifestation of a personal style? Do the drawings for the Glass House establish any distinction between Johnson's role in the breakdown of the International Style and that of the "advanced" American architects of the period, in particular Paul Rudolph, Minoru Yamasaki, and Eero Saarinen, each of whom

were hampered in their work by a far less comprehensive knowledge of history and a far more developed conviction of the moral rectitude of International Style modernism? The Glass House drawings do confirm one important point about Johnson the polemicist: that despite his polemical role in fostering Modern Movement architecture in America, he never saw this architecture or for that matter the Modern Movement as a moral or social issue; he was always interested in style but not in ideology.

The drawings for the Glass House reveal, in contrast to project sketches for many of Le Corbusier's early houses, Johnson's eclectic bias. While it seems obvious in the sketches for, say, the Villa Savoye, that Le Corbusier was not following a systematic or so-called rational line of thought leading to the final product, and that early schemes are quite unrelated to what was built, nevertheless, the differences in method reveal a fundamental difference in attitude. Le Corbusier's work is consistent from scheme to scheme; only the composition varies. Johnson's, on the other hand, is inconsistent. He experiments with a variety of forms while tending to compose in the same manner. Chiefly interested in stylistic experimentation, he undertakes no fundamental transformations of the initial spatial organization proposed: the grouping of the principal house and the guest house remains fairly constant throughout the process. Thus, each project of Le Corbusier's is ideologically charged while each of Johnson's seems an attack on the very idea of ideology, an essay in style.

There are exceptions to this rule. Scheme III (figs. 5, 6), for example, can be seen as a comment on Frank Lloyd Wright's Usonian houses of the 1940's: house and guest house are one, leading to a composition that seems distinctly related to the Lloyd Lewis House, a relationship that is substantiated by the evidence of the elevation. At the same time, the plan of the principal pavilion is different in composition from the earlier schemes; it is distinctly un-Wrightian in its organization and appears to be based on Mies's Resor House project of 1938—as sifted through the functionalism of Breuer's Binuclear Houses. This plan in turn seems to lead to the square pavilion scheme, which anticipates Mies's "50 × 50" House of 1950. From the point of view of spatial organization, this scheme is unique.

But uniqueness and eclecticism aside, the drawings for the Glass House present us with many problems that must be resolved. If the sketches confirm the idea that the Glass House is not wholly Miesian, then what is it? I have suggested that it is more a product of style than of ideology. Does it then reveal something about the in-herent character of Johnson? It is obvious that no easy answer can be found. More research will be necessary to probe the complexity of what previously seemed to be his most open gesture.

Notes

1. Johnson has donated ninety-six drawings of the Glass House to The Museum of Modern Art as part of an extensive archive established to document his career. Although not all the drawings are dated, Johnson recently numbered them according to a rough chronology he established based on recollection. This initial presentation of the Glass House drawings honors that chronology, although even a cursory glance suggests that there are some rough spots: for example, the sequence proposed for the summer of 1947 seems less a sequence than an expression of contradictory ideas held simultaneously—early testimony to the eclectic approach that has come to be regarded as characteristically Johnson's.

2. The Museum of Modern Art archive also includes thorough documentation of Johnson's student work at Harvard as well as a number of executed and projected buildings that precede the Glass House. These will be presented in a subsequent issue of *Oppositions* as part of an article, now in preparation by the author, "Philip Johnson's Architecture: The First Ten Years, 1939–1949."

3. Philip Johnson, "House at New Canaan, Connecticut," *Architectural Review*, vol. CVIII, no. 645, September 1950, pp. 152–59; reprinted in *Philip Johnson: Writings* (New York: Oxford University Press, 1978).

Peter Eisenman

From Philip Johnson Writings *(Oxford University Press), 1979*

I consider my own house not so much as a home (though it is that to me) as a clearing house of ideas which can filter down later, through my own work or that of others.

Johnson, quoted by Selden Rodman,
Conversations with Artists, 1957

From the Introduction to Philip Johnson Writings

Johnson is at his most transparent—the lucid ideologue—when speaking of his own house. Certainly his 1950 presentation of the Glass House at New Canaan in the *Architectural Review*[1] is an architect's way of presenting his own architecture. It is at once modest, straightforward, and telling. It is obviously the model used by James Stirling in his article "Stirling Connexions,"[2] which consists of parallel photos showing historical precedents and examples of his own work. But while Stirling seems interested in acknowledging what has preceded him, Johnson seems interested in the reverse, in creating a patrimony. It is now Johnson who, while following these precedents in time, by his particular use of them makes them seem as if he were the originator of their use.[3]

Here again Johnson deploys some of

what have been his continuing themes about the nature of architecture. For example, in his linking of ideal form to the intellectual revolution of the late eighteenth century, he places himself in a lineage of humanist abstraction, yet in his concern for the oblique angle of approach to a frontalized building and the play of asymmetric rectangles he forges an eclectic union that places his work even before the precedent of Schinkel's work. This essay on the Glass House is the first instance in which Johnson talks seriously, without his usually self-deprecating irony, the first time that he talks directly about the nature of his *own* architecture.

In 1965, in his article "Whence and Whither,"[4] Johnson further reveals this architectural paternity. He says, with his typically casual iconoclasm, that architecture is not the design of space, but rather the organization of procession; it exists in time. If one takes these two themes, space and procession, as the "brackets" of his words, then the Glass House in New Canaan and Pennzoil Place in Houston can be seen as the two poles of his work. They are in fact both preoccupied with the processional: the one pedestrian, the other vehicular. They are both glazed volumes of non-space, the one transparent glass, the other opaque glass.

From the Parthenon through Schinkel, Choisy, and the Beaux-Arts, architecture was concerned with corners, not fronts; with perspective, not axonometric views. In linking the oblique processional approach to the frontal appearance of the Glass House, Johnson is also countering one of the classical canons of the orthodox modernism of Le Corbusier and Cubism: in the modern canon, the façade was to be frontal, space was layered vertically and understood stereometrically, stress was at the periphery. The Glass House layers space horizontally, and its conception is from the diagonal.

In the traditional sense both Pennzoil and the Glass House are a-spatial; the latter is a void, and the former is a solid. But both lack the traditional energies—tension, compression, and so forth—that mark architectural space. They represent the beginning and the end of modern architecture. The Glass House is transparent and the carrier of metaphoric imagery;

Pennzoil is opaque, not metaphoric, not a polemic of the machine-made aesthetic, but rather the mute, unrelenting object itself.

It is only the steel wainscot line on the Glass House that violates this principle of a-spatiality. It turns the glass into a membrane—a container of interior space and not a void. But in none of Johnson's writings on his house can one find a discussion of this very crucial and untypical architectonic gesture, which differentiates him from the Mies van der Rohe of the Barcelona Pavilion and the Farnsworth House.[5]

But ultimately, it is not in the context of his patrimony that one must finally return to Johnson's presentation of his own house.[6] For me, it is in the context of something much more profound that this article and this house are fascinating. For it is here that text, building, and person fuse to shatter the paradox. And it is the casual text caption Johnson gives for his figure 17 in this article (see p. 14) that places the house and Johnson once and for all in a new context:

The cylinder made of the same brick as the platform from which it springs, forming the main motif of the house, was not derived from Mies but rather from a burnt wooden village I saw once where nothing was left but the foundations and chimneys of brick. (Johnson, "House at New Canaan, Connecticut," 1950)

How are we to interpret such a metaphor? Who builds a house as a metaphoric ruin? Why the burnt-out village as a symbol of one's own house? But further, that Johnson should reveal the source of his imagery seems the most telling of all: the Glass House is Johnson's own monument to the horrors of war. It is at once a ruin and also an ideal model of a more perfect society; it is the nothingness of glass and the wholeness of abstract form. How potent this image will remain long after all of us have gone, as a fitting requiem for both a man's life and his career as an architect! I know of no other architect's house that answers so many questions, has such a symbiotic relationship with personal atonement and rebirth as an individual.

In a more general context, the Glass House prefigures for me the parallel anxiety of post-World War II architecture. It remains the last pure form, the final gesture of a belief in a humanism so debilitated by the events of 1945. And at the same time it contains, in the image of that ruin, the seeds of a new conception of an architecture that is not for the reification of an anthropocentric man, but exhibits a more relativistic condition, a parity between man and his object world.

A successful monument, Johnson has said, should partake of the past and of the time in which it is built.

A glass box may be of our time, but it has no history. (Johnson, Statement concerning the Franklin Delano Roosevelt Memorial, 1962)

Johnson's writings, like his glass box, have the transparency of our time. It will remain for history to reveal their opacity.

Notes
1. "House at New Canaan, Connecticut" (see pp. 213–25).
2. *Architectural Review*, CLVII (May, 1975), pp. 273–76.
3. This is similar to the concept of surveying articulated by Harold Bloom in his book *The Anxiety of Influence* (New York: Oxford University Press, 1973) and later by Vincent Scully in his lecture on "The Shingle Style Today" at Columbia University, 1973.
4. See pp. 27–32.
5. This idea was first expressed by Johnson publicly in the three-part television series with Rosamond Bernier for CBS's Camera Three in 1976.
6. "House at New Canaan, Connecticut," op cit.

Craig Owens

From Catalogue 9, *September/October 1978*

*If philosophy is memory or a return of the origin, then
what I am doing cannot, in any way, be regarded as philosophy;
and if the history of thought consists in giving life to half-effaced
figures, what I am doing is not history either.*

The Archaeology of Knowledge, Michel Foucault

Philip Johnson: History, Genealogy, Historicism

In 1950, when Philip Johnson published his then recently completed Glass House, he compiled a miscellany of historical sources from which he claimed the Glass House had been derived.[1] The entries in Johnson's book of quotations ranged from the Acropolis and Ledoux's visionary projects to the painting of Malevich, Mondrian, and Van Doesburg, and the architecture of Mies van der Rohe. In their heterogeneity, the ancestors of the Glass House form neither a set nor a series; the former is composed of related or similar elements, while the latter arranges these in temporal or spatial succession. Johnson's sources are, by contrast, a dispersed collection of monuments which possesses no internal cohesion or logical order whatsoever; they do not demonstrate the solidarity by which we recognize a tradition.

In this text, Johnson effectively turned the popular conception of architectural modernism as anti-historical inside out to reveal a fundamental historicity at the heart of modernist practice.

Before proceeding, it is worth rehearsing the strategic logic according to which Johnson presented his sources. Before arriving at the Glass House, the reader encounters (1) a farm village plan by Le Corbusier from 1933 (fig. 3); (2) the Illinois Institute of Technology Buildings designed by Mies van der Rohe in 1939 (fig. 5); (3) Theo van Doesburg's "The Basso Continuo of Painting," (fig. 7) first published in 1922; (4) the Acropolis (fig. 8); (5) Karl Friedrich Schinkel's Casino in Glienicke Park, near Potsdam, ca. 1830 (fig. 1); (6) Claude Nicholas Ledoux's Maison des Gardes Agricoles at Maupertuis, ca. 1780 (fig. 6); (7) Mies's Farnsworth House, designed in 1947 (fig. 2); and (8) Malevich's "Suprematist Element: Circle" from 1913 (fig. 4). This order does not reflect any hierarchy of importance, but follows Johnson's "processional" view of architecture;[2] he thus began with the approach to and siting of his buildings before arriving at the Glass House itself. As a result, any ranking of sources, as well as any question of an historical development or evolution up to the Glass House, are suspended.

In dealing with what is an essentially historical question—what are the sources of the Glass House?—Johnson disregarded the most basic techniques of historiography: chronological succession and the historical process. The former links discrete events into the unbroken chain of a linear development, while the latter characterizes the present as either the natural or inevitable result of the interaction of autonomous historical forces. In Johnson's text, instead of the linearity of an unbroken chain there is a vertical system of correspondences, a projection in depth; instead of the cause-and-effect relationships of an evolution or development, a set of retroactive confiscations; instead of the singularity of an origin, a complex network of distinct and multiple elements, difficult to unravel; instead of the objectivity of the historian's discourse, the autobiographical *I*. This associative, mnemonic relationship to the past may appear to be *a*historical, since a history of the Glass House written

according to historiographical models would presumably have proceeded from the Crystal Palace through the Maison de Verre and Mies's Farnsworth House before culminating in Connecticut. Johnson obviously did not want to reconstruct that history—a refusal which demonstrates the fundamental anti-historicism of the modern movement. However, the relationship to the past as a dispersed set of monuments is not an annihilation of history; rather, it is an attempt to transform history into an entirely different mode of inquiry. The term *genealogy*, conceived by Nietzsche in opposition to history as it was written in the nineteenth century, describes this new operation.

Nietzsche criticized History as an attempt to capture essences; it assumes the existence of immutable forms which precede it and shape its course. Genealogy, by contrast, does not reveal ahistorical essences lying behind things or events, but the "secret" that things have no essence, or that what we call their essences were in fact "fabricated in a piecemeal fashion from alien forms."[3] Essences are historically constituted figures, and only as such are they admissible as objects of investigation. The genealogical study of essences thus has a deconstructive aim: if, in *Genealogy of Morals*, Nietzsche traced the descent and emergence of the concepts of good and evil, it was to prepare for their dissolution.

"There is no set of maxims more important to the historian than this: that the actual causes of a thing's origin and its eventual uses, the manner of its incorporation into a system of purposes, are worlds apart; that everything that exists, no matter what its origins, is periodically reinterpreted by those in power in terms of fresh intentions; that all processes in the organic world are processes of outstripping and overcoming, and that, in turn all outstripping and overcoming means reinterpretation, rearrangement, in the course of which the earlier meaning and purpose are either obscured or lost."[4]

Johnson's text on the Glass House describes precisely such a process of reinterpretation and rearrangement. According to the architect, a whole array of formal models were confiscated from history—he frequently uses the verbs *to copy* and *to derive*. By incorporating them into a new order, by recombining them with other, dissimilar elements, their original identities are submerged, subjugated to the roles they play in a new structure. Their "functions" are entirely dependent upon the position which they occupy in a new system. As a result, "the earlier meaning and purpose are either obscured or lost."

Thus, it no longer makes any sense to ask whether the glass house is original or derivative.[5] As Michel Foucault has stated, only objects which occupy the *historical* field may be classified as either old or new, traditional or original, "conforming to an average type or deviant:" "One can distinguish . . . between two categories of formulation: those that are highly valued and relatively rare, which appear for the first time, which have no similar antecedents, which may serve as models for others, and which to this extent deserve to be regarded as creations; and those ordinary, everyday, solid, that are not responsible for themselves, and which derive, sometimes going so far as to repeat word for word, from what has already been said."[6]

However, by parsing its materials according to the polar opposition of the original and the traditional, historical analysis, Foucault continues, "reinvests in the empirical element of history, in each of its stages, the problematic of the origin."[7] The new is original in so far as, in the absence of ancestors, it may serve as a model for future works—originality in the sense of seminality. Whereas the derivative is always derived *from* something; it is that something, in the form of an origin, which historical analysis seeks to locate.

However, in his text on the Glass House, Johnson effectively suspends the question of originality. The originality of the Glass House has always been compromised by the precedence of Mies's Farnsworth House, designed in 1945–6, but not built until 1950, after the completion of Johnson's project. We might be tempted to inquire which came first, but Johnson makes his indebtedness to Mies clear: "The idea of a glass house came from Mies van der Rohe. Mies mentioned to me as early as 1945 how easy it would be to build a house entirely of large sheets of glass. I was skeptical at the time, and it was not until I had seen the sketches of the Farnsworth House that I started the three-year work of designing my glass house."[8]

Despite superficial differences in elevation and plan—Mies's house is raised above the ground on stilts and painted white, while Johnson's hugs the ground, is black, and has a cylindrical core which, Johnson claims, Mies never would have sanctioned[9]—the resemblance between the two seems to have been the result of Mies's direct influence upon Johnson (Other preliminary working drawings show Johnson experimenting with other distinctly Miesian schemes; for example, the "court houses," which date to June, 1947, appear to be elaborations of certain of Mies's court house projects from the early 1930s). However, the Farnsworth House is the *eighth* source cited by Johnson. It is preceded by other, apparently less significant examples in which Johnson complicates the question of originality.

Earlier in the text, Johnson invoked another Miesian precedent: the relationship of the Glass House to its brick guest house and sculpture group was "influenced by Mies' (sic) theory of organizing buildings in a group. The arrangement is rectilinear but the shapes tend to overlap and slide by each other in an asymmetric manner."[10] These asymmetric rectangles are immediately compared with shapes which appear in Mondrian's paintings: "These shapes, best known to posterity through the painting of Piet Mondrian, still have an enormous influence on many other architects besides myself."[11] Among which Mies van der Rohe is presumably to be numbered. Significantly, Johnson does not illustrate this passage with a Mondrian, but with Theo Van Doesburg's "The Basso Continuo of Painting." If "best known to posterity through . . . Mondrian," why republish a Van Doesburg, unless it be to stress the fact that "The Basso Continuo . . ." was published by *Mies* in the periodical *G* in 1922? Re-enacting his predecessor's gesture—republishing the painting originally published by Mies—Johnson suggests that the "origin" for the arrangement of his buildings was not "original," but also derived from a source. By locating an origin within the origin, Johnson begins to trace its retreat.

We might also inquire into the relationship between Van Doesburg and Mondrian. Is one the source of the other? If so, which? The answers are not forthcoming; rather than a clear hierarchy of sources and derivations, Johnson proposes a complex network of relationships which does not resolve itself into the linear progression of a clear-cut development. This strategic retreat of the origin was prepared in Johnson's very first entry, in which an illustration of a farm village plan by Le Corbusier carries the following text: "The approach to the house through meadow and copse is derived from English eighteenth-century precedent. The actual model is Count Pückler's estate in Silesia."[12] Only later are we informed that it is the footpath between the Glass and Guest Houses that was "copied" from Le Corbusier. However, the question of Le Corbusier's relationship to picturesque models remains—and remains unanswered. By setting up the possibility of potentially infinite regress, Johnson subverts the methodological certainty of historical models. The mapping of antecedents does not guarantee a definite hierarchy of originals and derivations, causes and effects. Nothing carries "originality" with it as a property or quality; rather, "originality" is wholly a function of the system that is under scrutiny.

Johnson also undermines the criterion of resemblance, upon which historical relationships have, since the nineteenth century, been based.[13] On what ground may the Glass House be said to resemble its sources? Johnson's fourth entry depicts a plan and perspective of the Acropolis, reinterpreted for the oblique angle of approach to his buildings, as well as their arrangement so that only one would dominate the visual field from a given point. However, what Johnson interpreted was itself already an interpretation—of the principles of Greek city planning by the Beaux-Arts historian and archaeologist Choisy. Thus, "from the focal point at the beginning of the footpath near the parking lot, the brick house (Propylea) is passed and forms a wall on the right hand. The statue group (Athena Promachos) is in full view slightly to the right."[14] To complete the analogy, then, the Glass House becomes the Parthenon—not because they resemble one another, but because they occupy analogous positions in two similar systems. Analogy is not based upon resemblance, but upon *function*.

With the exception of Mies's works, there is no immediate resemblance between the sources cited by Johnson and his Glass House. Resemblances that may appear emerge only within Johnson's text, as results of the field in which Johnson situates his house. Resemblance is not a criterion of relationship, as much for, say, Schinkel's Casino as for the Farnsworth House. Even if the Glass House resembles the latter, this does not guarantee their identity. So that Johnson is not simply compiling a list of monuments which resemble his own work; rather, in tracing the descent of the Glass House, he is describing an effective field of appearance specific to it. He designates the set of conditions within which the Glass House operates: "One can no longer say that a discovery, the formulation of a general principle, or the definition of a new project, inaugurates in a massive way, a new phase in the history of discourse. One no longer has to seek that point of absolute origin, or total revolution on the basis of which everything is organized, everything becomes possible and necessary, everything is effaced in order to begin again. One is dealing with events of different types and levels, caught up in distinct historical webs."[15]

Such an acknowledgment of historical indebtedness constitutes neither a departure from modernism nor an anticipation of the more legible eclecticism that began to appear in Johnson's—and other architects'—subsequent work. Rather, the relationship to history as a collection of dispersed monuments is precisely that of the modernist work. Modernism emerged during the second half of the nineteenth century as, in part, a rejection of the rampant historicism of that century. And if *genealogy* seems to describe Johnson's strategies—and those of modernist works in general—it is because Nietzsche conceived genealogy in opposition to history as it was practiced in his time. Genealogy and modernism emerged at the same time and in response to the same situation; they were parallel phenomena.

Historicism developed out of Romanticism during the second quarter of the nineteenth century—but should we not say, with Foucault, that it "erupted," since the very notion of development implies unbroken continuity and is therefore thoroughly historicist? Historicism, "the first offspring of a rebellious sire [Romanticism], [was] more eager to accommodate itself to the world as given by common experience, less interested in innovation and change, a natural inheritor of the family business."[16] According to the historicist, history is a continuous, purposeful process; although the historian's materials are discontinuous figures—regions, periods, social groups, individuals—she or he links these together in unbroken chains of succession and thus in-

sures the passage from one to the other in a continuous thread. The historian's concerns are interstitial and unifying; an apparent discontinuity is transcended by relating similar objects to one another in temporal sequences.

However, historicism is not simply a method; it is also a philosophy which grants special privilege and authority to historical knowledge. For the historicist, the search for all intelligibility and value comes to an end in history. In *The Order of Things*, Michel Foucault traces the ways in which, during a progressively more historicist nineteenth century, history became "the depth from which all beings emerge into their precarious, glittering existence."[17] Indeed, the primary concern of that century was what has been called the wholesale "historicization of reality";[18] economics was transformed into a materialistic philosophy of history, biology into the history of evolution, linguistics into philology, and anthropology into the history of races.

The architectural practice of the nineteenth century was also profoundly historicist. Although the various Revival "styles"—Greek, Roman, Romanesque, Gothic . . . —which that century produced were sanctioned by a belief in certain immutable architectural essences which are manifested in all buildings,[19] according to Nietzsche eclectism was simply a mask for "the closely guarded secret of modern culture:" that the "culture" of the nineteenth century was in fact a fundamental lack of culture. "We moderns have nothing of our own. We only become worth notice by filling ourselves to overflowing with foreign customs, arts, philosophies, religions, and sciences; we are wandering encyclopedias . . ."[20]

Nietzsche diagnosed this condition as one of the excesses of the *historical* consciousness, which he identified as "the power of gradually losing all feelings of strangeness and astonishment and finally being pleased with everything."[21] Thus, historicism was also responsible for the various Oriental styles of architecture—Egyptian, Moorish, Indian, Japanese—which that century produced. These, in consort with historical revivalism, effectively dispossessed the Age of History of any claim to an architectural style of its own. Eclecticism effectively eradicated all of the *differences* by which we recognize and characterize styles.

The architectural domesticization of the strange and exotic had its counterpart in the profoundly historicist anthropology of the nineteenth century. If, at the beginning of our century, anthropology was to become "a discipline whose main, if not sole, aim is to analyze and interpret *differences*,"[22] then it had to divest itself of certain historicist notions—such as the unity of "mankind"—which had accrued to it during the previous century. According to Claude Levi-Strauss, historicism was an attempt "to suppress the diversity of cul-

ture, while claiming to acknowledge it fully."[23] Historicism worked to reduce all cultural differences to an historical dimension; although it works within the field of the discontinuous—history—historicism is wholly concerned with "closing gaps and dissolving differences."[24] Since Hegel, history was conceived as unified and cumulative. Western civilization, the most advanced stage of human evolution, thus preserved all other cultures within its memory and institutions. So that without stepping outside its own boundaries European culture was capable of comprehending the Other within the unity of its own development. However, this knowledge was possible only by means of a radical reduction: the Other was assimilable to Western culture *only* as an anterior stage of its own development. For an historicist anthropology, "primitive groups are survivals of earlier stages whose logical classification reflects their order of appearance in time."[25] Thus, cultural diversity was reduced to a temporal, i.e., historical, dimension; the only differences that remained were those of stages in a genesis.

In all of the arts, modernism emerged at mid-century into this atmosphere of rampant historicism. It was an acknowledgment of limits, a reintroduction of difference into what was conceived to be the continuous field of the same. Modernist literature revealed a fundamental unintelligibility to lie at the heart of the familiar; modernist painting deployed historical materials in discontinuous patterns which thwarted their synthesis. At the end of the century, the attempt to forge a new, and consequently different, ornamental style was overtly anti-historicist: Art Nouveau strategically inverted the crucial historicist distinction between nature and history, to which the historicist had attached exclusive importance.[26]

The modernist aspirations which followed Art Nouveau were international and futurist in scope. The activism of modern architecture was, in its beginnings, violently opposed to historicism which had come to be an instrument of power—historicism had "accepted the emergence of the bourgeoisie as an accomplished fact and then tried to halt history in place to prevent the release of the class behind it, the proletariat."[27] Modernism, focussed on the future, was an attempt to reanimate a defunct historical machine. This was not, however, in order to reanimate or restore the past; rather, like Nietzschean genealogy, modernism was fundamentally a clearing operation. The self-conscious relationship of the modernist work to its history is not preservative, but an attempt to clear a space in which the new might emerge. The activism of modernism was an attempt to substitute a principle of *acknowledgement* of the past for the passive *adaptation* of traditional forms. In this, it paralleled Nietzsche's attempt to restore a principle of activity to an evolutionary theory that stressed adaptation: "The democratic bias . . . now dominates all of

physiology and the other life sciences, to their detriment, naturally, since it has conjured away one of their most fundamental concepts, that of activity . . . Quite in keeping with this bias, Herbert Spencer has defined life itself as an ever more purposeful inner adaptation to external circumstances. But such a view misjudges the very essence of life; it overlooks the intrinsic superiority of the spontaneous, aggressive, overreaching, reinterpreting and re-establishing of forces, on whose action adaptation itself gradually supervenes. It denies, even in the organism itself, the dominant role of the higher functions in which the vital will appears active and shaping."[28] It is precisely this opposition of activity to *re*activity that motivates the modernist work of art, in which activity takes the form of an acknowledgement.[29]

If Philip Johnson's text on the Glass House stands as just such an acknowledgement of the architect's relation to history, this is an affirmation, rather than a contradiction of its modernity. To view the Glass House as either Miesian *or* romantic-classicist would be to situate it in terms of a logical continuity, a tradition. To see it, as Johnson encourages us to, as the result of an interplay of multiple, overlaping forces, is to perceive its fundamental modernism—original *and* traditional; autonomous *and* dependent. Johnson was not engaged in a recovery of the past; rather, operating within what was presumed to be a consolidated tradition, he demonstrated its fundamental heterogeneity.

If the radical dispersal of history which Johnson accomplished in his text on the Glass House underscores, rather than undermines, its modernity, the *assembly* of historical forms of the AT&T Corporate Headquarters pursues other ends. For AT&T is fundamentally preservative; Johnson has described it as a response to the antiquarian "spirit" of the seventies: "Today, we preserve everything—perhaps too much. But that is the feeling, the sensibility of our times."[30] However, the very notion of the "spirit" of an age—"which enables us to establish between the simultaneous or successive interplay of resemblance and reflexion, or which allows the sovereignty of the collective consciousness to emerge as the principle of unity and explanation"[31]—is itself profoundly historicist.

Johnson proposes a new "moral imperative": that architecture must be responsive to the *continuous* texture of the urban fabric into which it is insinuated.[32] It was precisely this sensitivity to the continuities of urban life which Nietzsche, in a short text "On the Uses and Abuses of History," distinguished as one facet of what he called "antiquarian history." Antiquarian history seeks the continuities of soil, language, and urban life in which our present is rooted and, "by cultivating in a delicate manner that which existed for all time, it tries to conserve for posterity the conditions under which we were born."[33]

The responsiveness of the AT&T Corporate Headquarters to a specific tradition of New York City architecture—McKim, Mead, and White, and Raymond Hood—is less a polemical statement, and more a personal one. For antiquarian history is the field of the personal, the idiosyncratic, the subjective: "The antiquarian is careful to preserve what survives from ancient days, and will reproduce the conditions of his own upbringing for those who come after him; he thus does life a service. The history of the town becomes the history of himself; he looks on the walls, the turreted gate, the town council, the fair, as an illustrated diary of his youth, and sees himself in it—his strength, industry, desire, reason, faults and follies. 'Here one could live,' he says, 'as one can live here now—and will go on living; for we are tough folk and will not be uprooted in the night.' And so, with this, he surveys the marvelous individual life of the past and identifies himself with the spirit of the house, the family, and the city . . ."[34]

Notes

1. Philip Johnson, *Writings* (New York: Oxford, 1979), pp. 212–26.
2. "Architecture is surely *not* the design of space, certainly not the massing or organizing of volumes. These are auxiliary to the main point which is the organization of procession. Architecture exists only in *time*. "Whence and Whither," in Johnson, op. cit., p. 151.
3. Michel Foucault, "Nietzsche, Genealogy, History," *Language, Counter-Memory, Practice*, trans. Donald F. Bouchard (Ithaca: Cornell Univeristy Press, 1977), p. 142
4. Friedrich Nietzsche, *The Genealogy of Morals*, trans. Francis Golffing (New York: Doubleday, 1956), p. 209.

5. The question of originality versus derivation has preoccupied Johnson's historians, particularly when writing about the Glass House. See, for example, Robert Stern, "The Evolution of Philip Johnson's Glass House, 1947–1948," *Oppositions 10* (1977).

6. Michel Foucault, *The Archaeology of Knowledge*, trans. A. M. Sheridan Smith (New York: Pantheon, 1972), p. 141.

7. Ibid., p. 142.

8. Johnson, op. cit., p. 232.

9. "The relation of cabinets to the cylinder . . . is more 'painterly' than Mies would sanction." Ibid.

10. Ibid.

11. Ibid.

12. Ibid.

13. "The method consists in taking the part for the whole; in concluding, because certain aspects of two civilizations (one present, the other past) bear *resemblances*, that there is *analogy* from all points of view. Now, not only is this reasoning logically unsound, but in a fair number of cases it is refuted by the facts." Claude Levi-Strauss, *Race and History* (Paris: UNESCO, 1952), p. 252. My italics.

14. Johnson, op. cit., p. 216.

15. Foucault, *Archaeology*, op. cit., p. 146.

16. Hayden V. White, "Romanticism, Historicism, and Realism," *The Uses of History* (Detroit: Wayne State University Press, 1968), p. 159.

17. Michel Foucault, *The Order of Things* (New York: Pantheon, 1971), p. 219.

18. The phrase is Karl Löwitn's, quoted in Berthold Riesterer, "Karl Löwitn's Anti-Historicism," *The Uses of History*, op. cit., p. 159.

19. Thus Ruskin: "I have long felt convinced of the necessity, in order to its progress, of some determined effort to extricate from the confused mass of partial traditions and dogmata with which [architecture] has become encumbered during imperfect or restricted practice, those large principles of right which are applicable to every stage and style of it." *The Seven Lamps of Architecture* (New York: Noonday, 1974), p. 10.

20. Friedrich Nietzsche, *The Use and Abuse of History*, trans. Adrian Collins (Indianapolis: Bobbs' Merrill, 1957,), p. 24.

21. Ibid., p. 45.

22. Claude Levi-Strauss, *Structural Anthropology*, trans. Jacobson and Schoepf (New York: Basic Books, 1963), p. 14.

23. Claude Levi-Strauss, *Race and History*, op. cit., p. 248.

24. Claude Levi-Strauss, *The Savage Mind* (Chicago: University of Chicago Press, 1966), p. 263.

25. Claude Levi-Strauss, *Structural Anthropology*, op. cit., p. 3.

26. However, when French Art Nouveau sought to consolidate its identity through legible references to Rococo sources in order to distinguish itself from its Belgian and German counterparts, it succumbed to both nationalism and historicism.

27. Hayden V. White, op. cit.

28. Friedrich Nietzsche, *The Genealogy of Morals*, trans. Francis Golffing (New York: Doubleday, 1956), p. 211.

29. "*Dejeuner sur l'herbe* and *Olympia* were perhaps the first . . . paintings in European art that were less a response to the achievement of Giorgione, Raphael, and Velazquez than an acknowledgement . . . of the new and substantial relationship of painting to itself. Manet produced works in a self-conscious relationship to earlier paintings—or rather to that aspect of painting that remains indefinitely open. They were not meant to foster the lamentation—the lost youth, the absence of vigor, and the decline of inventiveness—through which we reproach our Alexandrian age, but to unearth an essential aspect of our culture: every painting now belongs within the squared and massive surface of painting . . ." Michel Foucault, "Fantasia of the Library," *Language, Counter-Memory, Practice*, op. cit., p. 92.

30. Interview with the author, *Skyline* (May, 1978), p. 8.

31. Foucault, *Archaeology*, op. cit., p. 22.

32. "In a city with traditions, you not only can, but you should use them. I think there's a new moral imperative here . . . So it becomes almost a moral imperative to make your own work knit in somehow. It's like a buttonhook, isn't it? You reach down in and join in with things . . ." Johnson in an interview with the author, op. cit.

33. Nietzsche, quoted in Foucault, "Nietzsche, Genealogy, History," op. cit., p. 162.

34. Nietzsche, *Use*, p. 18.

The Glass House Revisited

Kenneth Frampton

From Catalogue 9, *September/October 1978*

The Glass House Revisited

Kenneth Frampton

Even before I built my pavilion, I was very much flattered by the following notice which appeared in the respected English magazine Architectural Design, *accompanying a picture of the model. The overtones of Puritan disapproval deriving from years of indoctrination in the "only-useful-can-be-beautiful" philosophy show that some of the British have forgotten their glorious eighteenth century heritage. We need more of this pointed, beautifully written criticism in this country!*

"One step further along the road to complete architectural decadence has now been taken by Philip Johnson, with yet another addition to his idyllic estate in New Canaan. Although it is passed off by the architect as a "folly," by virtue of its entirely false scale, it is, nonetheless, in its trivial historicism, quite typical of Johnson's recent work. This petit pavillon in pre-cast, sand-blasted concrete is situated on a podium in a hundred foot-long artificial "lake," upon which it raises itself to the grand height of six feet with aid of columns at less than three foot centers. It is indeed hard to believe that this is the same man who once designed and built the thirteen-year-old famous Glass House in which he still lives, or that a former admirer and collaborator of Mies can, in a few years, come to conceive such feeble forms as these."[1]

Aside from his bravura claim that the Glass House had been directly inspired by Mies van der Rohe's project for the Farnsworth House of 1947, Johnson revealed in 1950 the other cultural sources that had influenced the development of this work: on the one hand the eighteenth century Enlightenment line extending from Ledoux to Schinkel, and on the other the modernist syntax of the *G* group with whom Mies had been in contact in the early twenties—the Berlin circle of El Lissitzky, Viking Eggeling, Hans Richter, and Mart Stam. From the first came the idea of rendering the house as a pure sign, together with the notion of constituting its body in terms of an implied space. Both of these aspects are in evidence in Ledoux's Maupertuis house, where a spherical form lies poised in a recessed court as though it were the inner space-form of a monument whose primary mass had been magically removed. From this line also came the idea of

the loggia/belvedere as embodied in Schinkel's Glienicke Casino and later reinterpreted in Mies's Tugendhat House of 1930. From the *G* group came the Suprematist notion of "almost nothing"—a concept much beloved by Mies. On the other hand Johnson was also to take a most un-Miesian idea from the same quarter—that is, the idea of the circle in a rectangle which, as Johnson himself remarked, was too "painterly" for Mies. The location of the furniture in the Glass House and at a larger scale the spatial distribution of the glass and brick prisms—compositionally form and counter-form—across the domain of the site may owe something, as Johnson was to indicate, to Choisy's projection of the Athenian Acropolis or even, as he did not acknowledge, to Capability Brown for the oblique, curving driveway into the site. For the figure–ground incision of the paths into the greensward, Johnson claimed a rationalist precedence, as could be found in Le Corbusier's *ferme radieuse* of 1934, although Harvard Yard is also here. Finally, for virtually the same aspect of the composition, there is Johnson's acknowledgment of Van Doesburg's "Basso Continuo of Painting" published in the magazine *G* in 1922.

The Legacy of Mies: Court vs. Loggia
Schinkel's loggia/belvedere concept undergoes many transformations by Mies before it achieves its most condensed expression in the Farnsworth House. In this respect the same structural paradigm—namely, an eight column loggia—is present in the Barcelona Pavilion, the Tugendhat House, and the Farnsworth House (figs. 1, 2, 3). The interwoven theme of court house versus belvedere—all but totally abandoned in the Farnsworth House—is first fully synthesized by Mies in the Barcelona Pavilion where the loggia, part contained and part enclosed, looks out over the ruffled water of the outside pool in sharp contrast to the still, mirror-like water of the interior court. This opposition emerges more fully in the Tugendhat House where the romantic prospect of the garden and the city unfolds before the loggia/living room as a *natural* panorama, in contrast to the artificial winter garden of the adjacent conservatory. The Tugendhat "loggia" was unequivocally revealed in summer, when the retracted glass wall converted its living room into an *al*

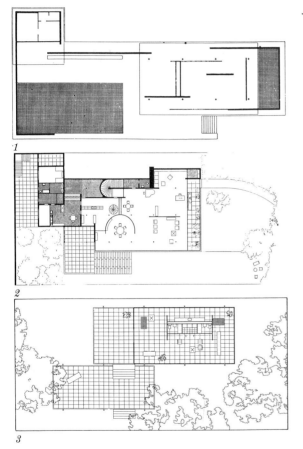

1

2

3

fresco belvedere (fig. 6). The chromium-plated balustrade to this loggia space is to re-emerge later as the horizontal chair rail in the Glass House, and it is here that the profound differences between Johnson and Mies first emerge, for where Johnson's chair rail has the same status as the fenestration of which it is an integral part, the Tugendhat articulates the separate status of each component; it differentiates the loggia into its necessary elements—the floor, the ceiling, the columns, the fenestration, and the balcony rail.

A more Neoclassical and less Suprematist version of the same theme is adopted in the Farnsworth House, where the fenestration is fixed and the loggia is established outside the glazed volume. This intent is confirmed by the structuring of the house and the entry podium where eight columns divide the concept into six supporting the house and two supporting the loggia. A reciprocal interaction is played out in the stub columns which support the entry platform, where four stub columns support the platform and two support the loggia. In the Glass House, on the other hand, the column system is partially concealed by the glass skin, so as to establish a hermetic glass box comparable in its phenomenological status to the brick Guest House. The "loggia" concept is now projected onto the greensward promontory itself, delimited on its edge by a low wooden guard rail.

Johnson was to follow the Miesian loggia/belvedere paradigm unequivocally in 1956 with his Leonhardt House (fig. 4), which was clearly a building of Mies's hillside house project of 1934 (fig. 5). However, where Mies is always *tectonic* Johnson is invariably *scenographic*. The relation to both nature and structure is in each case totally different. Like Caspar David Friedrich, Mies regards nature as an ambient mirage of light and verdure, a distant fusion of haze with the landscape or the near appearance of fossilized foliage miraculously suspended between floor and ceiling. For Johnson, nature—floodlit or otherwise—is nothing other than the picturesque. This difference is even more marked at the level of detailing, for where Johnson is indifferent to the means (providing the desired profile is obtained) Mies endeavors to establish within the

1 Barcelona Pavilion, Barcelona, Spain, 1929. Mies van der Rohe.

2 Tugendhat House, Brno, Czechoslovakia, 1930. Mies van der Rohe. Lower floor plan.

3 Farnsworth House, Plano, Illinois, 1947. Mies van der Rohe. Plan

4 Leonhardt House, Long Island, New York, 1956. Philip Johnson.

5 Sketch for a glass house on a hillside, ca. 1934. Mies van der Rohe.

6 Tugendhat House, Brno, Czechoslovakia, 1930. Mies van der Rohe. Section through the retractable window with winding gear.

4

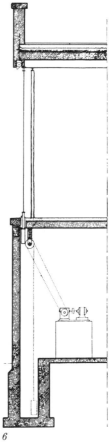

6

5

7 *"Fifty-by-fifty" House, 1951. Mies
van der Rohe. Axonometric.*

8 *Resor House, Jackson's Hole,
Wyoming, 1938. Mies van der Rohe.
Pencil and cut-out photograph. Note
the way the view is framed by the
structure.*

9 *Hubbe House, Magdeburg,
Germany, 1935. Mies van der Rohe.
Plan.*

10 *Farnsworth House. Section
through porch and podium stair.
Construction as ideal form.*

structure the same standards of elegance as are made manifest on its exterior. This would account for the diaphragm construction of the Farnsworth entry podium and loggia; an all steel welded deck in which twenty-four pyramidal drain pans support a travertine deck in such a way as to maintain a perfectly flat surface (fig. 10).

The Evolution of the Guest House
Although the eight column Farnsworth scheme was initially adopted by Johnson in September 1946, his subsequent rejection of Mies's structural logic seems to be evident from the evolution of the Glass House between 1946 and 1947. Thereafter, the house changed structurally from eight columns to four to six, the Syrian arch scheme occurring between the four and six column versions with Johnson rejecting the cantilevered corner which was essential to the Farnsworth eight and four column solution. This was the corner treatment which Mies was to adopt in his "Fifty-by-fifty"house of 1951(fig.7) and in his Farnsworth House completed in 1952. Johnson resisted to an equal degree the lifting of the house off the ground and Mies's provision of a Shinkelesque entry platform and loggia. In short, Johnson remained more preoccupied with the modernist aspect of Mies's early vision than with the Romantic Classicism that dominated Mies's later careers.

In deriving his Glass House *parti* Johnson was caught between a loggia/belvedere concept appropriate to the promontory site and Mies's prototypical court house (fig. 11) as embodied in his Hubbe (fig. 9) and Lange houses of 1925 and 1926 (See Scheme I; figs. 12, 13). Johnson had previously realized a Miesian court house in his Ash Street House, Cambridge, Massachusetts, of 1942 (fig. 38). Johnson's early sketches for the Glass House seem to be compounded in part out of Mies's Resor House for Jackson's Hole, Wyoming (fig. 8), and in part out of the Miesian court house—whose introverted form was patently unsuited to the site.

This dilemma is resolved in Scheme III (fig. 14) in which the notion of the introverted court house is abandoned and a pergola introduced to serve both as a link to the guest wing and as the frame to the vista over the valley.

In this case the living room attempts to address both the forespace or the virtual court, on the one side, and valley-panorama on the other.

In Scheme IV (fig. 15) the architect tries to return to the court concept more directly, only to abandon this strategy in Scheme XA (fig. 17) when the project begins to approximate to its final form of a glass prism poised on a bluff, looking one way toward the view and the other toward the forespace. And while its structure at this stage is the eight column Farnsworth format, the resultant space is structured not by a plane running down the length of the volume as this would have obstructed the view, but rather by the introduction of cylindrical forms for the bathroom and kitchen. Nothing could have been less Miesian, and for this resolution to the problem of maintaining a through-view over the valley Johnson was to be as much indebted to the vision of Malevich as to the primary forms of Ledoux.

The initial two cylinders linked by a serpentine wall, which appear in Scheme XA of September 1946 (figs. 17, 20), are eventually pried apart to achieve in Scheme XI (fig. 19) (November 1946) three separate cylindrical components which are rather diffidently used to structure the free space of the rectangular volume into dining, living, sleeping, and study areas. Thereafter, we are again witness to an effort to reduce the number of volumes to two, that is, to a hearth and a service core (see Scheme XII of April 1947, fig. 18), and then to a single cylinder combining both fireplace and bathroom, thereby leaving the kitchen to float as a free-standing work-top (see scheme dated November 1947, fig. 32).

In the late spring of 1947 the whole project is reworked into a wall house with the main living room looking over the valley on one side and the Guest House on the other (Scheme XIII; fig. 24). In June 1947, Johnson attempts to resolve the courthouse/belvedere conflict in a more condensed manner (Scheme XIV, fig. 23) by arranging for the bedroom of the main house to open onto a court (cf. the Barcelona Pavilion), leaving the living area to open to both the entry court and the valley. The Guest House

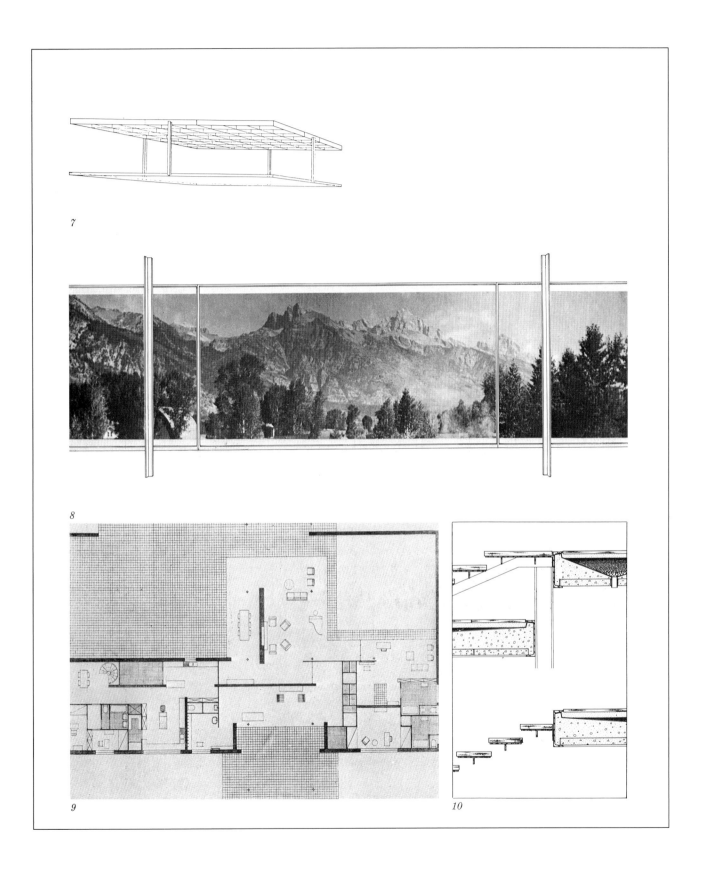

7

8

9

10

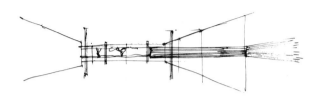

11

*11 Project for a Court House, ca.
1931. Mies van der Rohe.*

*12 Glass House. Scheme I.
Elevation.*

*13 Scheme I. Plan. Belvedere/house,
loggia, and guest house.*

*14 Scheme III. Plan and elevation.
Note resemblance to Mies's Kröller-
Muller house.*

*15 Scheme IV. January/February
1946. Plan.*

12

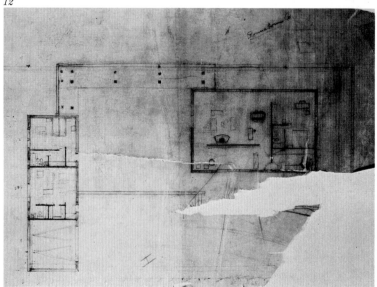

13

emerges as a free-standing brick box in Schemes XVI and XVII (figs. 22, 21) and with the exception of a brief flirtation with the so-called Syrian arch parti Scheme XX (figs. 25, 26, 29) it is to remain in this solid and opaque form as a foil to the Glass House. Scheme XVII of June 1947 (fig. 21) seems to have been Johnson's last attempt to link the guest and main houses through the treatment of the paving; the main house is already being treated as a symmetrical, self-sufficient form with one entry door in the middle of each façade.

The Resor House paradigm is returned to for the last time in Scheme XXIII (fig. 30) as a means of orienting the living volume to both the entry and the view; this parti being definitively abandoned in favor of a glass prism in October 1947 (figs. 31–35). The resolve in this last series of sketches is simply a matter of using a cylindrical rather than a rectilinear core.

The Celestial Elevator

Nothing could be more Suprematist than Johnson's likening his Glass House to a "celestial elevator in which when it snows, you seem to be going up because everything is coming down." This paradox of word and fact suggests the modernist attributes of work as built. The conceptual conflict between the belvedere and the court house was to be finally resolved by treating the whole bluff as a court house on a mini–acropolis, in which the trees surrounding the house serve as the perceptual limits of the domain. These limits are unambiguously established at night by floodlit trees, while during the day the domain is determined by the extent of the manicured lawn, the *tapis vert* upon which the *open* and *closed* boxes are nothing but revealed chambers within a much larger conceptual but "invisible" domain of domesticity.

But aside from such vestigial references to the belvedere and the courtyard the Glass House achieves its ultimate *jeu d'esprit* by being a box within a box within a box. Thus, as in Johnson's New York apartment, designed by Mies in 1930 (fig. 37), the classic furniture of the Glass House finds itself contained within a carpet, which sits in its turn on the podium of the house itself, on a base which

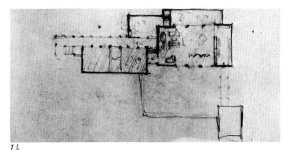

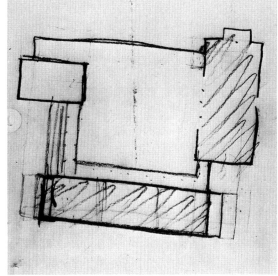

14

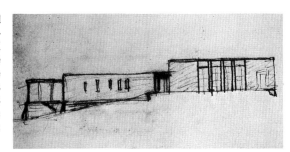

15

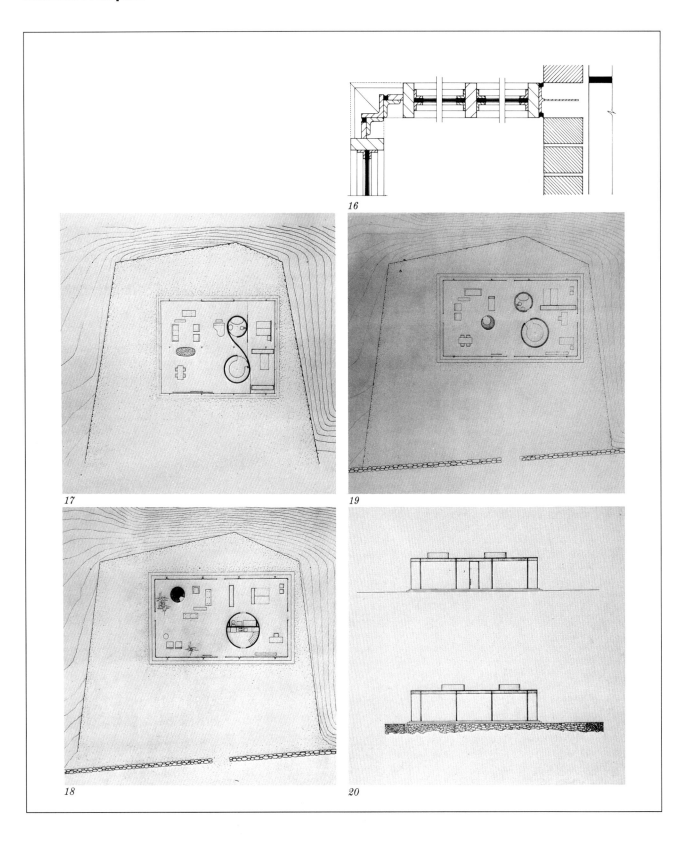

16 Glass House fenestration. Combined corner and sill details.

17 Scheme XA. September 1946. Site and floor plan.

18 Scheme XII. January/April 1947. Site and floor plan.

19 Scheme XI. November 1946. Site and floor plan.

20 Scheme X. Elevations.

21 Scheme XVII. June 1947.

22 Scheme XVI. Site and floor plan.

23 Scheme XIV. June 1947. Plan.

24 Scheme XIII. May 1947. Plan. This version is virtually a wall house.

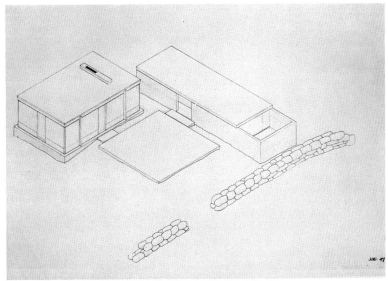

21

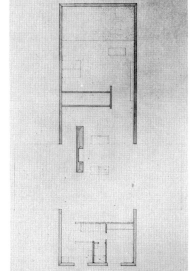

23

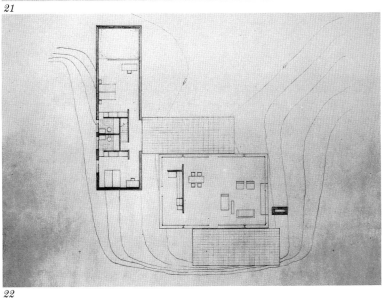

22

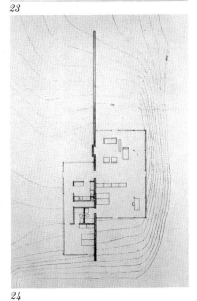

24

25 *Scheme XX. The so-called Syrian Arch scheme. Elevation.*

26 *Scheme XX. Sketch elevations.*

27 *Scheme XXIV. Elevation.*

28 *Scheme XXIII. Elevations.*

29 *Scheme XX. Plan. The Syrian Arch scheme.*

30 *Scheme XXIII. Site and floor plan.*

31 *Preliminary corner detail study. Not executed.*

32 *Final plan. November 1947. Site and floor plan.*

33 *Penultimate plan. October 1947.*

34 *Miscellaneous plan studies.*

35 *Plan, elevation, and structural variation. October 1947.*

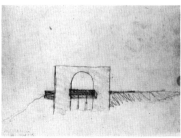

25

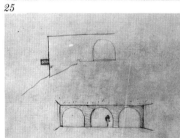

26

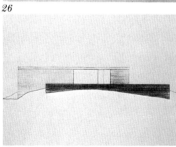

27

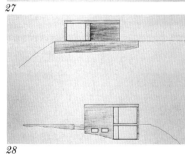

28

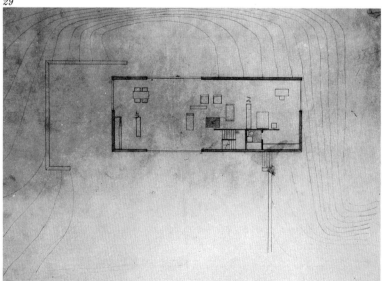

29

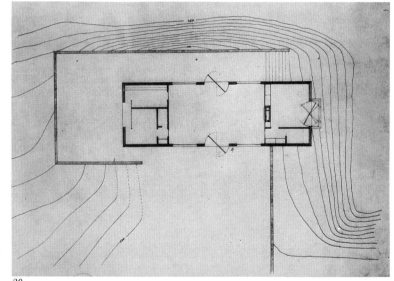

30

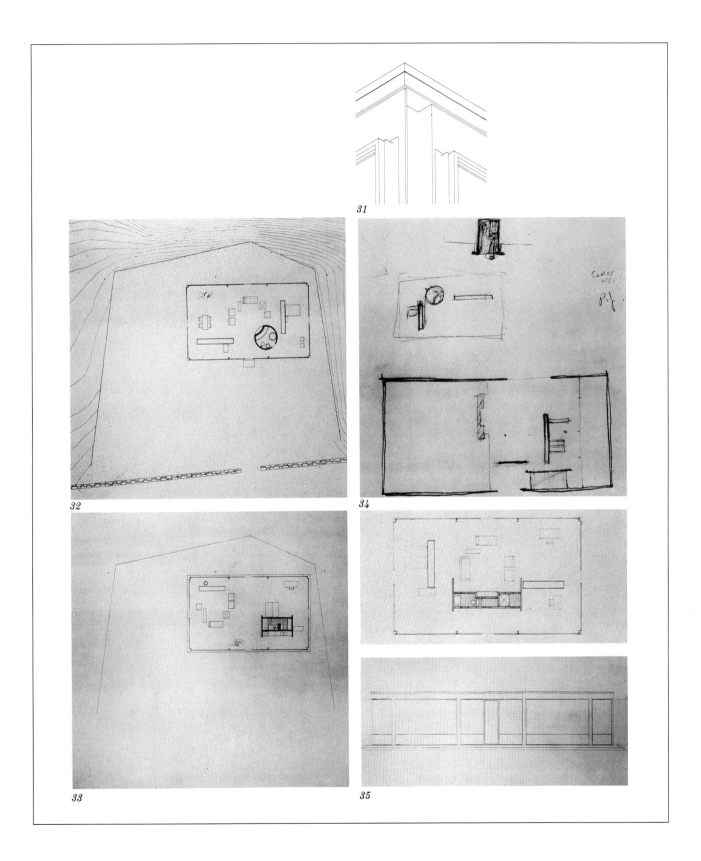

31

32

33

34

35

*36 Ash Street House, Cambridge,
Massachusetts, 1947. Philip
Johnson. View through courtyard
at night.*

*37 Architect's apartment, New York
City, 1930. Designed in part by Mies
van der Rohe.*

*38 Ash Street House. Aerial
perspective.*

36

37

38

is evidently yet another carpet, this time of woven brick-work set within the tapis vert of the clearing.

The subtlety with which the Glass House is detailed stands in strong contrast to the naivete of its development. In its detailing it is as removed from the Miesianism of Johnson's Ash Street House as it is from the banal project that Johnson made for an equally Miesian glass structure to be built in the garden of the Museum of Modern Art in 1948. The strong phenomenological impact of the Glass House on the other hand stems from its *suppression* of its structural system, that is to say from the fact that the glass membrane and the steel fenestration are set more or less flush with the outer surface of the prism so that unlike the Farnsworth House no shadow is cast onto the skin from the free standing columnar frame. The hermetic sides of the box are reflective, refractive, or transparent depending on the light—but they are never shaded by structure. This skin-tight proposition has other corollaries for the conceptual order of the house; for where the expressed exterior columns of the Farnsworth House serve to stress the isolated horizontal planes of its floor and ceiling, Johnson's Glass House is ordered about a brick cylinder which pierces the roof slab in such a way as to emphasize the autonomous status of the roof plane. The surface of the podium, on the other hand, is treated as an earthwork, its woven brick herringbone fusing (through the identity of the material) with the brick cylinder of the bathroom/chimney core. This is the fulcrum of Johnson's metaphor of the incinerated house, to which he referred in 1950 when he wrote: "The cylinder, made of the same brick as the platform from which it springs, forming the main motif of the house, was not derived from Mies, but rather from a burnt-out wooden village I saw once where nothing was left but the foundations and chimneys of brick. Over the chimney I slipped a steel cage with a glass skin. The chimney forms the anchor."

These laconic words not only suggest that the Glass House was based on the vision of a ruin, but that the ruin in question was almost certainly the blitz-krieged remains of a village. It may well be, as Peter Eisenman has suggested, that the Glass House is Johnson's cryptic monument to the horrors of war; that here beneath the flowers of Xanadu lies embedded the petrified remains of a lost ideal and an elegy for the dead. Equally indebted to both Mies and Malevich the status of this house as a work of art derives from its capacity to synthesize many diverse sensibilities at once. It is equally rich outside the affinities of any particular style, and as our perception passes from one subtle inflection to the next it is successively prism, loggia, earthwork, ruin, and tent. And yet is not this sophisticated intersection of many strands a final closure of bourgeoise utopianism, a definitively reductive modernity, a folding in of humanism upon itself, the state of solipsism raised to unparalled elegance, the end of a trajectory rather than a beginning?

Note
1. Philip Johnson, quoted in an article on the building of his pavilion in New Canaan, in *Show Magazine*, 1963. The latter quote from *Architectural Design* of the same year was written by Kenneth Frampton, then Technical Editor of *AD*, and published without a byline.

39

40

41

GLASS HOUSE

SCULPTURE

GUEST HOUSE

39 Glass House, and Guest House and pool. Site Plan.

40 Glass House and Guest House. Model.

41 New Canaan Estate, Philip Johnson. Early site plan of Glass House, Guest House and provisional siting of the pool.

42 Glass House and Guest House.

43 Glass House and Guest House.

42

43

44 *Glass House as belvedere. Guest House to the left.*

45 *Glass House in Winter.*

46 *Glass House in Spring.*

47 *Glass House. Plan.*

48 *Glass House. Interior. Note the "woven" brick floor.*

44

45

46

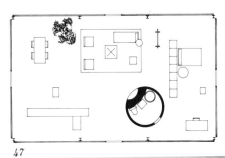

47

48

49

50

51

49 Glass House. Interior.

50 Glass House. Passageway leading to study space. Entrance to the right, bathroom to the left.

51 Glass House. Bathroom interior.

52 Glass House.

53 Glass House.

54 Glass House. Detail of built-up roof and steel fascia construction.

55 Detail of corner junction between fenestration and structure.

52

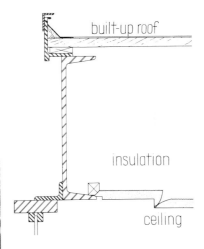

54

53

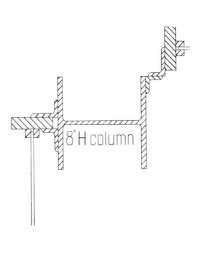

55

56

56 *Glass House.*

57 *Philip Johnson.*

58 *Guest House. Plan.*

57

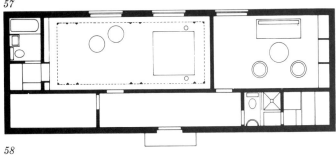

58

Francesco Dal Co

From Lotus *35, 1982*

The House of Dreams and Memories:
Philip Johnson at New Canaan

Maurice Blanchot has noted how, after Worringer, certain "German painters directed plastic art towards the study of a field without any privileged points and which presents no possibility of orientation, developed through motions in which every point possesses the same value. Subsequently, Klee dreamed of a space in which the total omission of the centre would simultaneously suppress every trace of the vague and irresolute."

An analogous procedure, which we can imagine as a tendency towards "release from the centre," appears in the "pavilion system" which Philip Johnson has been constructing for his own home in New Canaan, Connecticut. The first phase of this set of buildings goes back to 1949 and was the famous Glass House. It was followed by the guest house, the pond, a gazebo on the pond and two galleries for Johnson's private collection, and, more recently, the library.

The New Canaan complex has all the features appropriate to the dwelling of a collector—even if, in this case, it happens to be a somewhat special collector; one whose character has one element in common with that "prototype" of the contemporary collector, Eduard Fuchs, whom Benjamin immortalized in his portrait of this remarkable "collector and historian."

Johnson, too, in his home in New Canaan, combines collecting and "historicism," even though this "historicism" takes an eminently autobiographical turn. Johnson's art-collecting is united with architectural collecting. But it is, precisely, an encounter between different tendencies. In cataloguing his own architectural works,

Johnson distances himself from them in order to "appraise" them, setting them in what is virtually a historical perspective. With critical detachment, he proceeds in this way to the construction of his own architectural biography. This operation presupposes an outward projection, a "division" of the self. This is a split which the collector mends by creating his own collection of works of art. In the latter case the "historian" no longer intervenes; the object studied is no longer represented by autobiography. Satisfying one's taste is different: it requires a work of self-identification. This empathy cannot serve a person who instead narrates his own work: to do this it is advisable to attempt to place oneself outside one's investigation and order the results with the eye of the "historian."

This detachment is illustrated by the sequence of buildings on the New Canaan estate. The process they define is that traced by the split which separates them from the author of their story. They represent the account of a process leading to the accentuated contestation of the *centre* from which the collector started. The conquest of a space without a centre links certain aspects of modern art with the aspirations of the collector. The latter partly shares the tension that Blanchot mentions; he cultivates temptations to expansion of possession which is achieved in the extreme detail of the forms through which possession itself is fulfilled.

This "progress beyond the centre" is another essential aspect of the buildings conceived by Philip Johnson for himself at New Canaan. They trace out a series, from the Glass House to the very recent library. This building knows the secret of surprise, evidence of indubitable intellectual vitality. That this evolution should be interpreted as a demonstration of the *Ichspaltung* to which the person who started the movement has to be subjected is confirmed precisely by his autobiographical vocation.

The Glass House is both a tribute and a farewell. Johnson himself has fully clarified its autobiographical character, displaying its intellectual "history" in ways similar to those which a chemist might use in describing the phases of a process of synthesis or distillation. This does not contradict the fact that the Glass House is an act of homage and farewell. Johnson produced this refined "glass box" in the years when, as he has recounted himself, his name might as well have been Mies van der Johnson . . .

Generally in his writings Johnson keeps strictly to the rules of fair play. He carefully clarifies the sense of his studies, rejecting any attempt at mimicry—yet mimicry is one of the keys to his architecture. Is the little gazebo by the pond puzzling? Does it provoke the moralism of critics? Narcissistic nonsense perhaps? The answer is simple. It comes from Johnson himself. To complete the Glass House—and there are no other apparent reasons —first a pond was *needed*, and then, to enrich the pond, the gazebo was *needed . . .* As can be seen, what counts is always "the need for completeness": autobiography and collecting require continual expansion. In architectural terms, this leads to a progressive obscuring of the centre, from which the whole of the composition originates. In being completed, the Glass House becomes encircled. It is no longer a "centre," but just the initial item in a collection which will have to be continuously enriched. Says Johnson: "I had a pond—two years ago the place needed a pond—which looked rather empty. Something interesting to look at from the house was necessary. Contrarywise, some place to walk to from the house—from which to look at the house—was also necessary."

From this—from this yearning for "completeness" by which to appease every nascent "necessity"—is derived the progressive effacement of the original order established with the layout of the Glass House. The "disorder" of the inner composition is accentuated, as the detachment from the glassy fixity of the first "box" appears as an architectural route through autobiography. With this, the dialectic between order and disorder, between centre and periphery, between certainty and uncertainty, becomes the key of the architectural tale Johnson is offering us. From this emerges the labyrinthine character which the entire system ends up by acquiring.

The construction of the "home" as labyrinth—once Johnson complained of the lack of attention shown by contemporary architects for the ancient art of gardens, and of course one of the typical expressions of this art was the designing of mazes—embraces the entire metaphor of the biography narrated in architectural terms. The labyrinth is derived from, among other things, its own peculiarity of the simultaneous presence of the enigma and the keys to solve it. This is a mechanism which one also comes across in his autobiography. The solution of the biographical enigmas requires a continual probing of information, an ever-wider collation of facts, a broadening of perspective—but in every case it relates to a possible "solution."

The extension of facts and informations is what is represented by Johnson in the buildings constructed at New Canaan. They are conceived as a succession of different architectural episodes, recomposed only conceptually in the proper order as metaphors of an equivalent number of phases in the sphere of autobiography. This sequence starts from a separation in the form of a tribute. The Glass House marks the departure from the language of Mies, from a truly demanding "tradition." Few contemporaries have been so involved in the decline of the tradition of the *modern* as Philip Johnson. Few have felt the burden of the "Miesian" past as much as Johnson has, or had the courage to pursue that course to the point where they glimpse the last bridge with its broken arches. The

Glass House looks onto this break in the old highway and reacts to it with an almost imperceptible yet decisive difference. It is at this point that there begins an experience that is the reverse of that Johnson had lived through until the 1950s. A new relation with tradition is established. This was heralded with the presence, in the heart of the rarified geometry of the Glass House, of a cylinder of masonry, appearing in that context as an anti-Miesian heresy. From this heresy there stems a new dialogue with the languages of the modern past. It is a relationship that now begins to develop in prevalently destructing terms. Deconstruction, from this point on, will strive to dismantle and break up even the most solid idioms which contemporary architectural languages had succeeded in fashioning.

Deconstruction implies a continuous decodification. Johnson is aware of this to the point of applying it to his own works, attaining the form of the autobiographical essay through the accumulation of "relics" at New Canaan. This need to decodify is combined in Johnson's work with the eclectic experimentalism of his formal research, with the autobiographical narcissism which is one with the innate penchant for collecting.

It is no accident that the metaphor of the labyrinth should have been favoured. In this form there appears to co-exist the tendency towards expansion peculiar to the collector and his yearning for decipherment: possession becomes necessary for the solution of the enigma, but this already presupposes the presence of him who will succeed in violating it. In the case of the New Canaan estate, this ideal picture proves complicated and completed by its autobiographical implication inherent in the architectural plot. This relates to that "historicist attitude" which is always typical of the collector. This web means that the constructions of New Canaan are always subject to continuous expansion. By reproducing them, the architect sublimates the coherency of his own research, the integrity of his intellectual experiences, the redemption of his lost freedom—freedom pushed to the frontiers of autobiography. But each further chapter in this tale confirms its labyrinthine nature. Each new project renews an interplay of reflections; it enriches the plot with further complications requiring new solutions.

This strategy of sublimation is, however, exposed to a twofold contradiction. The "reality" is in fact excluded from the labyrinth, whose centre remains the enigma. If this were not enough, the now known succession of Johnson's buildings constructed at New Canaan could bear witness to it—the early tributes to Mies, and then the pond, the interplay of false scales expressed through the gazebo and the two antithetic galleries: one need only take a look at the latest building, the white library, a felicitous intuition which hovers elegantly between elementarist allusions and impressions from Le Corbusier's formal poetry, and this will be confirmed. The library once more covers his traces. It is a passage that seems related to the forgotten origins of the journey. An episode that seems to seek a remedy for the inadequacies of the earliest "chapters" of the autobiography, but, at the same time, on the purely architectural plane, it is a fertile insight; almost seeming to express that while it may be advisable to enter into conflict with the modern, this by no means excludes the need to recognize the breadth of this past, its richness, the ignored challenges which are still concealed in it.

With the construction of the library, finally, the whole complex at New Canaan acquires a mature bodily fullness—even though the work of the collector is probably not at an end. At this point, however, the "home" which Johnson desired for himself appears sufficiently detailed. But herein lies the confirmation of the contradiction we have spoken of. This "home," in fact, represents the apotheosis of the interior. The *interieur*, in Benjamin's sense, appears in it as the direct product of the need that drives the architect to widen his collector's avidity to the point where it is satisfied even by an autobiographical narrative. The *traces* which Johnson hides in his home are the same signs as those that segment his autobiography. This induces him to devote himself to the primacy of the interior. His strategy can only be opposed to that which Benjamin takes over from Brecht when he warns the "inhabitant of the big city" of the need to go systematically about cancelling his *traces*.

But if it is the *interieur* that has to be saved, the destiny of the home proves to be determined by this fact. It can no longer appear as a *monument* in the strict sense; instead of being a house it will therefore be a celebration of the story and the autobiographical memory which animate the *interior*. But together with this the interior exacts a sacrifice. It imposes the adoption of solid protection against the *exterior*, while by its architectural nature it exposes itself to a destiny which tends to reverse the sense of its autobiographical sublimation. The protection of the interior which Johnson pursues is secured in two complementary ways. On the one hand, this is achieved by accentuating the "processional" character that distinguishes the modes of relationship between the buildings constructed within the estate and the external environment. This tendency appears even in the arrangement of the Glass House: it is the formal nature of the glass box, as Philip Johnson himself explains, that imposes a distorted, "oblique," "detached" approach. In the second place, the interior which contains the "tracks," which is treated as a "monument" architecturally indicating its diversity from the context, lends itself (precisely by means of this twofold order of reasons: *interior* and *monument* are two expressions of the collector's mode of being) to being fundamentally a *museum*.

Ernst Jünger has grasped the affinity which "exists between the realm of the museum and the great cult of the dead and of graves, and in this regard the museum confesses itself the legitimate child of the monument. In technical language, all these things are 'munuments' . . . and their staff are 'keepers': a name which suggests the relation between the museum and the process of mummification." The traces which the vocation for autobiography disseminates throughout the interiors of New Canaan, in pursuit of its own expository clarity, are exposed to this same danger. The traces of the collector here tend to become mute relics. In this way they confirm the closeness of their link with the *interieur*, with the "home" understood as a private shelter in which to live, with this ultimate expression into which modern investigation of the sense of the monument seems destined to withdraw. This radicalizes the separation of the exterior that the architectural treatment anticipates in its rejection of the context. From this there stems a tax-onomic organization of settings forming the "home" in New Canaan. The "protective strategy" which Johnson intended to adopt in building his dwelling for life finds its conclusive expression in this arrangement.

Like the guests in New Canaan, housed in a special building detached from the original Glass House, the other architectural episodes are also scattered about the rest of the estate, following their own formal inclinations. Just as the Guest House is intended to safeguard the integrity of the Glass House, so the subterranean picture gallery and the pavilion of sculptures arrange in sequence the various experiences that the "home" can offer, taking good care to present them separately. The fruit of Philip Johnson's vocation as a collector, the two galleries have not only the function of explicitly introducing into the home the character which the *interior* has been implicitly acquiring (that of the museum), but also perform the function of preserving the interior from the danger that the outer world might interfere with these "tiny oases of marble and gold," while *evoking* their presence in the ironical or disconsolate sublimations of pop-art kept in the galleries. Only as art, uniquely adopted within this aura, is "life" permitted to violate the interior of New Canaan; but at the same time, "life" can only be represented in a fashion suited to these *interieurs*: adopted by collecting, it is sublimated as art and set below underground domes.

There may be various different keys to explain this story. Many approaches appear for an understanding of the superimposition of levels on which this singular autobiographical tale is developed. But one of them is, perhaps, the way by which to free oneself from the feeling of egocentric narcissism which, to a superficial impression, is emanated by what Johnson has constructed for himself in New Canaan.

In one of his finest writings, Johnson has declared: "Now we know that we cannot 'solve' anything. The only principle that I can conceive of believing in is the Principle of Uncertainty." True, this is not an original statement . . . but it is original to hear it from a designer like Johnson. New Canaan is the "museum" of his uncertainties. It is no accident that the Glass House, with the passing of time, has been losing its value as the centre of the composition that Johnson has imposed on the taxonomy of his interior. This is the "museum" of what might have been but wasn't. It is the place where the collector protects his own difference, keeps the fruits of his curiosity, "studies the world" (both the "external world" and the world animated by the forms of his imagination as architect), allowing it to filter strictly through the barriers protecting his "historian's" workshop—the "historian" of himself first of all— . . . and hence the symbolic significance of his last building, the library.

A completely private world, New Canaan does not admit basic explanations apart from the autobiographical purpose which Johnson has poured so liberally into these buildings. What emerges is a remarkable museum of architecture. True, this is an architecture represented in keeping with the tastes of a single collector and conceived by a single designer—but in this "museum" the uncertainties, the rules violated, the baseless games, the uncertainties, the extra-territorial nature of contemporary architectural languages, are ruthlessly listed, memorized and catalogued.

As a great admirer of Jünger, Hans Slemayer, states: "The world, for which the museum is becoming the most sacred theme, is already, by its essence, a world which sees everything in a historical perspective." Philip Johnson probably belongs to this world as well. For this reason he possesses a trait in common with Georg Fuchs. His collector's spirit reaches New Canaan, where it narrates synchronically the story of contemporary architectural *uncertainties*, arranging in the *museum* they give shape to, the traces of the interior of his own life as well.

Walter Wagner

From Architectural Record, *July 1983*

Architect's Retreat

"I can't work in a glass house. There are too many squirrels running around outside." So Philip Johnson built this tiny study/library, the sixth building (after the house, the guest house, the pavilion, the painting gallery, and the sculpture gallery) on his 40-acre property in New Canaan. "Everything about this little building helps me concentrate. It's a three-minute walk from the house, and that helps. The space is just right (about 15 by 20 feet with a 10-foot ceiling), the light is glareless, the colors are gentle, I'm surrounded by books, and I can't be distracted by anything going on outside. I find I spend six hours there almost every Saturday and Sunday—in two-hour stretches, to be sure, since that's about as long as I can concentrate and besides there's no . . . well, there's no water."

As to "references" and "allusions," Johnson says, "I have been trying to work some out ever since the building was finished. Some see an Islamic influence—dome and minaret. Others see a play on solids and voids—the glass house, of course. And still others have decided I wanted a sculptural object in the middle distance—which I guess it is. I don't think any of that is right—I just wanted a place to work and to explore some ideas in space and scale and light that interest me."

The scale of the building is, of course, purposely unclear—indeed falsified by the overscaled 4- by 6-foot window and oversize entry, a 3- by 7-foot door let into a 5- by 10-foot wooden panel. The major light source is the oculus—3 feet in diameter at the top of its cone and capped with double glass, 10 feet in diameter at the ceiling line.

("There's a historical reference for you. I did try to figure out why the oculus in the Pantheon is just the size it is.") Three 1$^1/_2$- by 4-foot skylights wash the faces of the books with light. The window is dark glass, so there are no shadows or glare and except on the brightest days it reads as a picture on the wall—"no distractions."

The walls of the building are 10-inch concrete block, finished outside with a cement-base waterproof coating and inside with 2 inches of rigid insulation and plaster over metal lath; the cone is laid up with 8-inch concrete bricks similarly insulated and finished; the floor is wood-framed. The roof slab is more complicated—it is 8 inches thick, rather elegantly reinforced and poured with a 3-foot-deep concrete ring stiffener to support the load of the oculus.

And so, in several ways, it might be said of this small and simple building that its simplicity is really only skin deep.

View from the brick facade of the Guest House, 1950.

The domed Pink Room in the Guest House, 1953. "Cloud of Magellan" by Ibram Lassaw, 1953, is over the bed; Fortuny fabric is on the walls and ottomans covered in lambswool were designed by Johnson.

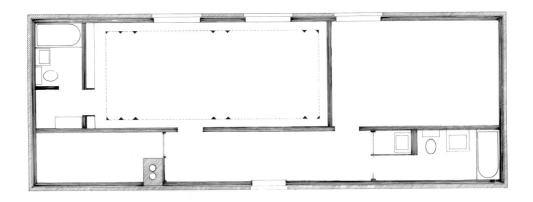

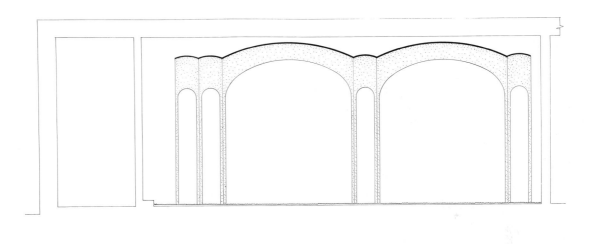

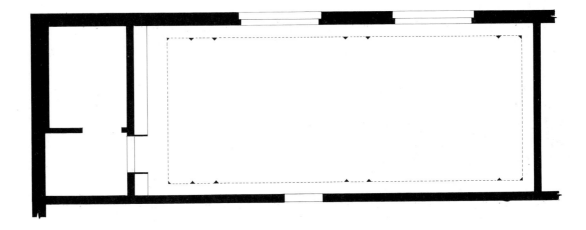

Top, *plan of the Guest House showing the location of the Pink Room.*
Bottom, *plan and section of the Pink Room. This represents Johnson's
first departure in design from the original Glass House elements.*

The Pavilion with the original 120-foot jet of water, 1962 (the jet has
since been removed). Johnson has written about this building that it
was "big enough to sit in, have tea in, but really right only for four-foot
people."

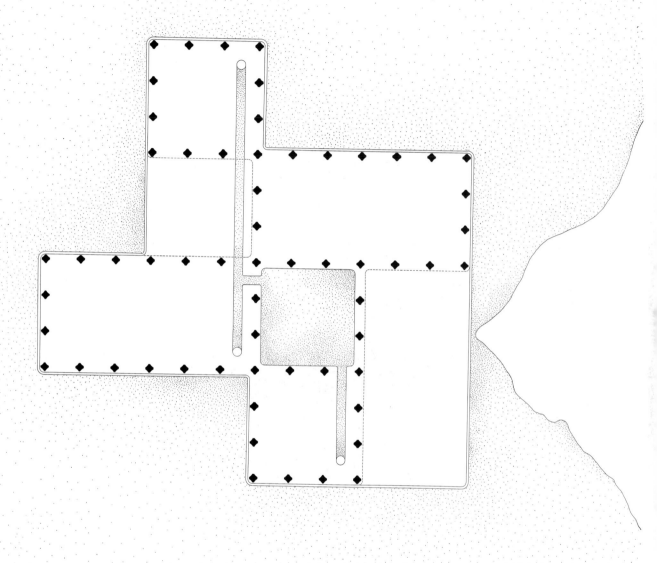

The plan of the Pavilion, 1962.

*The Painting Gallery; "Untitled" by Robert Bart, 1967, is on the left,
and through the doorway is Jasper Johns' "Flag," 1954-55.*

*In the Painting Gallery on two panels that revolve around a central
column*, left to right, *"Untitled V," Willem de Kooning, 1982;
"Untitled XIX," Willem de Kooning, 1977.*

In the Painting Gallery, left to right, *"Konskie III," Frank Stella, 1971; "Endpaper," Jasper Johns, 1976; "Summer," Jasper Johns, 1975; "Common Reader," David Salle, 1981.*

In the Painting Gallery, left to right, *"Julia Warhola"* Andy Warhol, *1974; "Self-Portrait," Andy Warhol, 1966; "S & H Greenstamps," Andy Warhol, 1962; "Lady, Dog, Lizard," James Rosenquist, 1985.*

Top, *site plan of the Painting Gallery, 1965;* bottom, *plan of the Painting Gallery showing the revolving panels on which the paintings are hung.*

The entrance to the Sculpture Gallery with, outside, *Julian Schnabel's "Ozymandias," 1989 and,* inside, *Roy Lichtenstein's "Glass III," 1977.*

In the Sculpture Gallery, top level, *"Lovers on a Bed II,"* George
Segal, 1970; right, *"Empire II," Robert Rauschenberg, 1961;* far
right, *"Prismatic Flake #4," Michael Heizer, 1990;* center, *"Untitled"
(in three parts), Robert Morris, 1965-70;* foreground, *partial view,*
"Raft of the Medusa, Part I," Frank Stella, 1990.

The interior of the Sculpture Gallery with, far left, *a partial view of "Neon Templates of Left Half of My Body Taken at Ten Inch Intervals," Bruce Nauman, 1966; center, "Raft of the Medusa, Part I," Frank Stella, 1990; foreground, "Untitled" (in three parts), Robert Morris, 1965-70.*

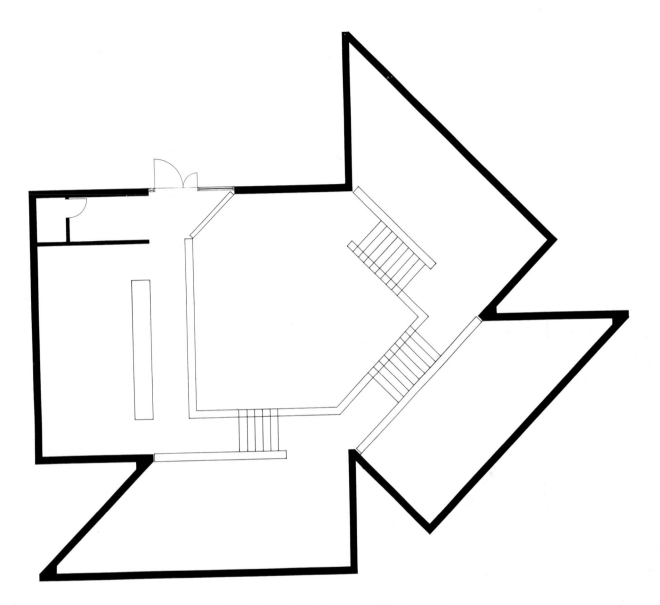

Plan of the Sculpture Gallery, 1970.

The Study, 1980.

Interior of the Study with skylit bookshelves. The room is sparsely furnished with a 5' × 5' table and three chairs. "I don't invite many visitors into this space . . . it is really a place for one man to concentrate."

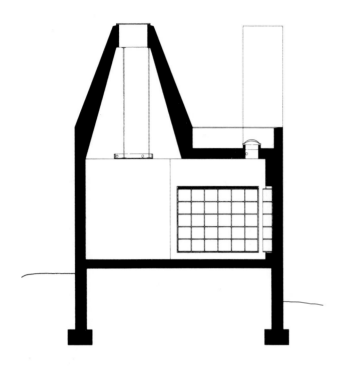

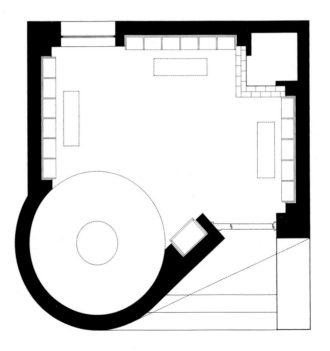

Top, *section of Study,*
bottom, *plan of Study.*

Entrance gate to the compound with electronically operated bar, 1977.

*The Lincoln Kirstein Tower, built in 1985 on the side of the pond
and named in honor of the poet and founder of The New York City Ballet.*

The Ghost House, an homage to Johnson's friend Frank Gehry, who is known for his use of chain link fencing. In the summer, liliums grow in it, protected from the deer.

Rosamond Bernier

From House & Garden, *June 1986*

Improving His View

Philip Johnson is at this moment just about the most visible American architect there has ever been. In some American cities it's quite a neat trick to be out of sight of one of his buildings, and if there's a dinner table where he never turns up in conversation I would like to hear about it.

But this ubiquitous and ever more controversial near-octogenarian has a secret side—one he rarely talks about but never ceases to act upon. He is a dedicated, compulsive, almost obsessional landscape architect.

No one has ever hired him to do it. It is done on his own property in Connecticut, and in his apparently nonexistent spare time, and he has been at it for well over a quarter of a century. "All landscape architecture is hopeful architecture," he said just the other day, and he knew from the very beginning that it would take a while to work with the hand that nature had dealt him. But if you live in a glass house, as he does, you have to do something about the view from the windows.

"When I first came here," he said, "the landscaping was all second growth, with a few old trees. The undergrowth was so dense that it took me twenty minutes to walk here from the road, though it's only a few hundred feet. The real-estate agent couldn't believe that anyone would buy a piece of land like that, buried in the woods. But I could see, though he couldn't, what trees I could cut and what a view I could get.

"Southern Connecticut is really one of the great landscapes, because it rolls at exactly the right degree of humanistic pleasure. Not quite as good as Ireland, of course. Ireland is the greatest. A landscape has to have the right folds at the right scale. Big folds don't do you any good, because then you're lost in the heights. Little folds are no good, because they're too small to give you a sense of containment. Ohio, where I come from, has folds, but it doesn't have folds in hills. Southern Connecticut has exactly the right change in grades. We're one hundred twenty feet, in this place, from the road to the pond that I created down there. It's very graspable, one hundred twenty feet. Then there's a ridge, a mile or a mile and a half away, which is just the right height. Again, that ridge contains the view.

"So I could see the potential of the five-acre slice, the good old American slice with its narrow part on the road. I could see where I could sculpt it, after I'd cleared it, and gradually I found the knoll where the house was going to be, and now is. The knoll at the time was deep in the woods where nobody could see it. So I cleared the field from the road down to where I was going to build the house, and I cleared enough to see the great tree that was going to be the anchor for the house. No one could see that tree, even in the winter, but I knew it was there.

"The great English landscape designers—Capability Brown, Humphrey Repton, had it easy. They started with fields, and they could see what they were working with. I lived here for five or ten years before I even saw the row of maples that now make the path to the art gallery. I never knew they were there, the underbrush was so dense. It was nineteenth-century underbrush, by the way. People always say 'eighteenth century,' but I always, consciously and infuriatingly, say nineteenth, which sounds better to me and worse to them. As I bought more land, the landscape became like a negative cutting into raw wood. Jefferson must have done that, because that's what Monticello was like before he got there.

"One thing I learned early on. My adviser said, 'Look, it's *never* a mistake to cut a tree.' I was horrified at the time, but I went ahead—cutting, cutting, cutting. I still cut down fifteen or twenty trees a year. I realize I shall be in trouble with the local nature lovers, but I have to free us from the terrible curse of New England, which is the tree. New England is a jungle, and it has to be beaten back, just as the Brazilian jungle has to be beaten back, though not quite as often. You don't have lianas to swing on, like Tarzan, but it crawls up to meet you.

"Americans don't understand woodlands. They let second growth come up. They let little trees and shrubs come up that entirely blind you. In any French or German forest you look under the tree trunks and see dappled shade. There's no such thing as dappled shade in American forests. I worked very hard to get dappled shade. Forest ferns are the greatest things you can have. The more I make the dappled-shade theory work, the more the forest ferns make the great floor.

"As stupid as Americans are about trees, their grandfathers were very good about walls. The old stone walls of the eighteenth century, the farm walls, were made because you couldn't plow the fields for all the rocks. So you took the rocks, and you piled them, and you made the wonderful walls that now make delineating and orienting lines on this property.

"We have almost too much water in Connecticut. It's like the jungle. The hillsides are full of springs and rivulets. I made the mistake of bulldozing one rivulet that I thought I didn't want, and all the trees that were anywhere near it died. So I bulldozed it back again, and it became the brook that I bridged on the way to the gallery—one of the most important parts of the landscaping. It's incredible, the mistakes one makes. But the point of landscaping is that you have to feel your way. It's amazing how the great English designers knew where to dam lakes and refix them to come out right. They must have been marvelous engineers.

"Back home in Ohio, my mother carved a pond out of a lazy old creek. So I said I'd make a pond, too, right here. Doesn't everyone? I made the pond, and I designed the little pavilion down there that I wanted to put in water. Now I want to make the pond bigger, so it almost fills this immediate valley and goes up the hill on the other side and is dominated by the tower."

The tower in question, made of concrete blocks, is named after Philip John-son's lifelong friend, Lincoln Kirstein. Few of us can climb up it as fast as Philip Johnson in his eightieth year, but fundamentally it is not so much for climbing as for looking at. It is a scale-creating, shade-creating object.

The bone-white gateway that leads off the road is, like the tower, something that arouses our curiosity and focuses our attention. Philip Johnson doesn't like our attention to wander. "That's why I don't like the seaside. There's nothing there, unless it's a boat. If there's a boat, it's O.K. In the East River wonderful barges go by. But God keep me from the Atlantic Ocean. There are a lot of glass houses that face the ocean, and people like them. But I say there's nothing there. You have to have buoys or floats or anchored boats or something, like St. Martin's, where there's a washed-up derelict ship, a marvelous hulk, all rusted, quite possibly dangerous, but at least you have something to look at. Anyhow, the pavilion and the tower and the water here reflect differently all the time, so at least you have something to look at."

There is also "something to look at" in the gateway that Philip Johnson built a few years ago. "All English houses have interesting or impressive gates to announce their presence. It's having to open them that's a bother. So our engineer devised a way of making the gate rise and fall by remote control from the car. Don't ever do it, by the way. It breaks down all the time. But I had to start somewhere. It furthered my technical education, and it serves as a piece of sculpture and as several other things besides.

"I don't want to 'decorate' the Connecticut landscape. It's perfect as it is. I just take advantage of the thirty-five acres that I now have to create interesting distances and points of high interest in a small amount of land, where you can't think in terms of three hundred sixty degrees and go on forever as the Sun King did."

All this could spring from a local, limited passion—a passion aroused and confined to a small, given part of a very large country. But as a matter of fact Philip Johnson has large and unlimited views on this subject, as on most others. "When *The New York Times* asked me what was the greatest piece of architecture in the world, I said the Ryoan-ji garden in Kyoto. There isn't even a building in it—just a porch, with the sky as its ceiling, and some rocks set in the sand. I wish it could be put into words, and yet it's good that there are some things that cannot be put into words. When you're in the presence of really great art there are no words. You can explain the role of the Madonna in Western art—Meyer Schapiro can talk about it, anyone can talk about it—but I've never met anyone who can talk about a pile of rocks. Why does that pile of rocks do that to us? That's very strange. But perhaps it's true of all architecture, and I think that we should stretch the definition of architecture to include landscape architecture, because we

always have the sky and the trees, or whatever there is, to work with."

English landscaped parks count for much with Philip Johnson, but he hasn't seen many. "I get it all from books, of course. In any case the English park has been ruined by the rhododendron. Rhododendrons kill architecture. All the great landscape architects knew that. If you put in a bush, it's a dead stop. Whereas a grove of trees has penetrations and holes in it. A bush is a dead subject." Thereafter followed a characteristic Johnsonian aside, to the effect that in any case the best English garden was in Wörlitz, near Dessau, in East Germany. Reference to a Baedeker for the year 1913 confirmed that there is indeed an English garden in Wörlitz. Laid out between 1765 and 1808, it includes lakes, islands, a monument to Venus, a Gondoliers' House, a Pantheon, and a "Grotto for Egeria."

"Goethe loved that garden. You have chain bridges that you clank your way across. You have mountains that you walk through, with a little piece of red glass as the only source of light. You have lakes that you pull yourself across in a little scow with a rope. It was a dead-level place, so they built a ridge of hills, always on a slightly small scale, so that you felt a sense of containment, not being able to go directly from here to there. The whole thing was built from nothing."

Though tempted at that point to eulogize the mighty Wörlitzer, and to imagine his Gothic, neoclassical, and Venetian elements transported to southern Connecticut, I was immediately brought back to more familiar ground. Landscape gardening was a matter of keeping up the interest as one walks along, Philip Johnson said. "The Tuileries gardens prove that. If you walk from the Louvre to the place de la Concorde along the dead straight rue de Rivoli, it's quite a long walk. But in the Tuileries you have the green bits, and the square squares, and the round rounds, and trees here and sculptures there, and it's not a bit boring.

"My garden is a combination of American Frontier, Moderne architecture, the English garden, and the lake and the willow. But it's the whole layering that matters, with the wilderness coming and going, and the ruins of the old barns and the old farm walls to give a sense of history. That is what has made the spirit of the place live on. And then the dappled light—a re-creation of the primeval forest and the hopeful growth of the floor of ferns, and the groves that I've planted."

A look of young man's mischief came over Philip Johnson's face. "Take my word for it," he said, "this place will look just great in a hundred years."

Vincent Scully

From Architectural Digest, *November 1986*

Philip Johnson: The Glass House Revisited

This year marks Philip Johnson's eightieth birthday and the thirty-seventh anniversary of the building of his Glass House in New Canaan. As it was originally constructed, that house was laid out in a modest clearing in Connecticut's second-growth woodlands, accompanied only by its complementary Brick House, with a sculpture by Jacques Lipchitz on the lawn between them. The setting was fundamentally suburban. Houses in wood by John Johansen and Marcel Breuer were to be found not far away.

Johnson's house was distinguished from theirs by the permanence of its materials and the classical order of its structure, by the minimalist discipline of its simple shape, and by the relative formality of its plot plan as a whole, but it was still, like the others, a suburban house set out alone

in nature and unsupported by any coherent system of garden design. Oaks, ash and maples stood close around it and covered the rest of Johnson's extensive holdings. It was the age-old American house in the woods, but plate glass, steel and central heating had enabled it to cast off its exterior sheathing and to stand psychologically open to the trees.

Like its Colonial forebears in Connecticut, which had been English in derivation, the Glass House was a European import, somewhat simplified and regularized in response to American conditions but based directly on the work of the European Mies van der Rohe, especially on his first American residential designs, the Resor House in Wyoming and the Farnsworth House in Illinois. It stood as an aloof pavilion among the trees, supremely confident in its technology, like American culture as a whole in 1949. And since it was seen mainly hemmed in and from close by, it looked very large, high and generous in its proportions. Johnson planted a big white pine alongside the entrance axis to enhance that effect, and the world soon began to beat a path past it to Johnson's glass door.

Frank Lloyd Wright came during his last decade: "Do I take my hat off or keep it on? Am I inside or am I out?" Mies himself arrived, furious with Johnson for "misreading" his steel details and stamping out into the night when Johnson asked him a question about his admiration for Berlage of forty years before. All the architects came, and every student who could make it, and for over twenty years Johnson kept open house, leading an ongoing architectural seminar and supporting what was in effect the most sustained cultural salon that the United States had ever seen.

While this was taking place, Johnson himself was growing. As for most Americans at that period, his growth was sparked by travel. In 1952—inspired perhaps by the work of the great classicist Frank E. Brown at the American Academy in Rome, and by Eleanor Clark's *Rome and a Villa*, dedicated in part to Brown— Johnson visited Hadrian's Villa and other Roman monuments, and the results soon began to be seen in his work. The bedroom in the Brick House got a hung Roman vault, a vehicle of light like Hadrian's vaults, but most of all Johnson's vision of his house as a whole began to reach out to embrace the surrounding landscape, as Hadrian had done at Tivoli. The trees began to go down, each one wept for (every visiting student appalled at the carnage), and the long ridge above the house was cleared.

An axis like one of Hadrian's, parallel to that of the longer dimension of the Glass House but far away from it in space, was now directed along the ridge, with ancient Rome and medieval Italy deployed upon it. A painting gallery was dug into the uphill slope, mounded over with grass-growing earth like a Mycenaean tomb. Its plan recalled those of Hadrian's nymphaea, but beyond them, deep in time, lay Malta's Neolithic temples, shaped like the earth goddess, and Calypso's cavern on Gozo in the center of the sea, where Odysseus was offered immortality if he would renounce his wife and home.

At the end of the path, inspired in part by hill towns such as those described by E. M. Forster in *Where Angels Fear to Tread*, Johnson laid out a building in the form of a brick stairway, lighted through a roof entirely of glass. It contains his collection of sculpture, spaced along the stair and tigerishly striped in Sienese bandings of shadows cast by the skylight above.

Now the landscape had become too vast to be defined by the Lipchitz; it was sold, to be replaced by a circular swimming pool of dubious effect. Then, below the Glass House, Johnson ruthlessly attacked the forest, clearing the trees off the steep slope, which turned out to be made up of gigantic boulders at Giulio Romano's titanic scale. Below them Johnson laid out a large pond of irregular shape, like those in English Romantic gardens. Now for the first time Johnson began to think of the landscape as a whole in terms of traditional garden design and particularly that of the Picturesque garden. He therefore built his first true Folly, just offshore in the pond, as if floating on the water. It was a kind of gazebo-colonnade, an abstracted temple so small that Johnson could barely stand up inside it. That trick of scale made it look much farther away from the Glass House than it actually was, while a skyscraping jet of water was made to burst up out of the pond beside it. A general scheme of exterior lighting also came into play, dramatizing all the relationships and unifying the garden architecture at night.

So things rested for a while, until Johnson set upon the woods south of the house. Out in the empty meadow that resulted he placed his most problematic Folly of all: a little abstract white-stuccoed building, adrift in space. Its disoriented geometry called up the haunting work of Aldo Rossi, along with some of Rossi's own sources in Boullée's conical chimneys, with their sinister contemporary reminiscence of death-camp crematoria. Here Johnson does much of his work at present; his desk is lighted by the flue and offers a view down the slope toward a series of old foundations that line the valley floor. These are the remains of farm buildings, and Johnson is constructing a little chain-link

structure over each one—suggested, he says, by the work of Frank Gehry, but also reminiscent of memorial buildings by Rossi and Robert Venturi. The garden thus begins to take on something of the character of a cemetery.

Perhaps in recognition of this, Johnson has erected a rather funereal entrance pylon on the public road above the study. Its flanking piers are finished in the same hard white stucco, while the aluminum tube of the lintel between them is set just low enough to prevent the passage of trucks and to cause a momentary uneasiness in the drivers of automobiles.

But the most striking new Folly of all, and the one most suggestive of the passage of time, is the open stairway, the gray ruined tower of cubical concrete blocks, which now rises on the far slope above the pond and the gazebo. It is intended as a tribute to Johnson's friend Lincoln Kirstein, for whom Johnson built his fine theater for the New York City Ballet at Lincoln Center. It recalls the Gothic ruins in English gardens, and as such it complements the classicizing colonnades of the water temple below it. It has something of Mies's ominous Monument to the November Revolution in it as well, but it is most like one of Escher's ambiguous, in-and-out, upside-down prints. It is indeed a little frightening to climb, narrow, unexpectedly high, and devoid of handholds as it is.

From its summit, also unexpectedly, one can see for the first time that Johnson has neighbors. Suburban houses show up on the skyline, and some lurk quite close among the trees. There are other settlers out there. The chimney of a burned house emerges from the forest. Now is brought home to us with renewed force something that is in fact inescapably apparent from the moment we pass beneath the entrance pylon: that Johnson has laid the site bare to its bones. The scattered trees now stand isolated on the naked body of the land, and we are made to see the truth of Connecticut: that it was once all farms. Their old stone walls now run unmasked across the rocky landscape, which is as hard and stern as that in *Ethan Frome*. But it is also bigger and more challenging than we normally think of it, in its arboreal softness, as being. It is in fact the American continent in its Colonial guise, the way it was in late Colonial early republican times.

The English lake down below now looks inconsequential, and its fountain irrelevant. We sense more than ever before that the site is high. The west wind sweeps over it from the Berkshires; we feel the whole continent roll. On it the Glass House, once ample, is tiny. The individual is small on the hard metal of the earth,

but he is tough enough to open to it all.

In 1947 Johnson gave the first lecture that identified the importance of Taliesin West to America. His place now joins, as no one thirty years ago could ever have thought it would, not only Taliesin West but Monticello too as a major memorial to the complicated love affair Americans have with their land.

Of those monuments, Johnson's is the most modern. The strongly orchestrated axes of the other two do not control the landscape. Johnson's buildings are all formally distinct from one another, marking the random growth of the alienated modern individual as he tries to find his place in America and in time. His residence's most compelling pathway, however, is the one that runs along the ridge above the Glass House. One feels the whole lie of the land most fully from there. The path ends in the sculpture gallery, against the far wall of which, right on the axis, terminating the whole landscape, a piece of sculpture by George Segal is placed. It is an old iron bedstead, flaked with age. Two lovers lie on it, wraiths in white plaster, pillowed on the contour, naked to the stars.

View, opposite, *of the compound from the Pavilion, 1986.*

Joseph Giovannini

From The New York Times, *July 16, 1987*

Johnson and His Glass House: Reflections

"All architects want to live beyond their death," said Philip Johnson, sitting in the living area of his Glass House in New Canaan, Conn., reflecting on why he has given it to the National Trust for Historic Preservation. "There's room for 12 houses on the land—I'd rather preserve it than have a ticky tacky subdivision built. And I'd like to build up a national trust."

Philip Johnson, for nearly 40 years the owner of the Glass House, which he designed for himself, has recently become its tenant: in December he completed negotiations, started in the 1970's, to transfer the house and grounds to the trust.

While the 81-year-old Mr. Johnson still spends his weekends there—dining and reading in the Glass House, sleeping in the brick guest house opposite, working in a small library in a nearby meadow—his estate of eight separate structures has be-come one of 18 National Trust properties.

He has the right to occupy the house as long as he wants, but when it eventually opens to the public it will be the trust's only abstract modernist building, and its only home designed by an architect for himself. A built record of Mr. Johnson's ru-minations, the complex will be an Ameri-can equivalent of Sir John Soane's house and museum in London.

Dressed casually in a sweater, and wearing rubber boots because he had just walked across the wet meadow from the study, Mr. Johnson spoke of the house, its history and his life in it as he sat on a Mies van der Rohe chaise longue, among Mies chairs, in a glass-and-steel building itself inspired by Mies. The furnishings in the open-plan, free-span house had not been changed or repositioned since he placed them there 38 years ago.

It was just after World War II and Mr. Johnson, as director of design and architecture at the Museum of Modern Art, was working with Mies on the approaching show of Mies's work when he was introduced to the possibility of a glass house. "Mies had mentioned to me as early as 1945 how easy it would be to build a house entirely of large sheets of glass," Mr. Johnson said. "I was skeptical."

For three years he worked on a design, and in 1949 completed the structure along with a brick guest house. The Glass House was symmetrical, serene and entirely enclosed in glass—the surrounding woods could be seen through glass panes that themselves reflected the woods. Anyone in the house essentially occupied the landscape; Mr. Johnson went to bed with deer watching.

Because he was his own client and willing to live in an architectural ideal uncompromised by conventional notions of privacy and convenience, he was able to create a pure Miesian vision: a classically proportioned frame with meticulously detailed, finely proportioned steel limbs. "More Mies than Mies," the Princeton architect Michael Graves has said.

The press and students came; the house was a celebrity even before its first bath in Windex. It attracted the oracles themselves, Mies and Frank Lloyd Wright.

"Mies thought the workmanship was bad, that the design was bad, that it was a bad copy of his Farnsworth house, which had inspired me," Mr. Johnson said. "He thought I should have understood his work better." Mies also disapproved of the fact that the ceiling joists were of wood.

Wright, walking through the front door, asked whether he should take his hat off or leave it on.

Like a lightning rod, the house has drawn critics and controversy over the decades. "By surrounding his house with all glass instead of much glass, Philip Johnson has stepped through the mirror," wrote the editors of *Architectural Forum* soon after the house was finished.

Serge Chermayeff, a professor of architecture at Yale, said, "Imagine living in a house where you carry the garbage out the front door."

Jaquelin Robertson, an architect in New York and Charlottesville, Va., has said that it was the only estate in America built in a modern style.

The house attracted many guests, and for about two decades the animated, opinionated, insatiably curious Mr. Johnson held a salon. Open-glass-house, however, finally came to a stop, he said, "with my wish to work on weekends." The architect normally lives in the city during the week and uses the house as weekend retreat.

While the Glass House never changed, everything around it did—the property became a canvas and a laboratory. "I learned that a pavilion in the woods is suffocated by the trees," he said. "They close in. The wallpaper needed pushing out."

Mr. Johnson bought several adjacent parcels of land and started to build other structures in the reaches of the new property, designing the grounds to make a picturesque landscape with borrowed views and several meadows on several levels. He created a small lake at the bottom of the rock shelf on which the house sits. Thinning the trees revealed the old stone walls of the original farm land.

He added a miniature pavilion of columns in the lake in 1962, an earth-berme "underground" gallery in 1965, a white sculpture gallery with a glass roof in 1970, a walled study under a conical roof in 1979, a monumental free-standing staircase in 1985 and, most recently, a ghost of a structure: a tulip cage made of chain-link fencing set atop the foundations of a ruined farm building. All the habitable structures other than the Glass House have solid masonry walls with very few windows.

A veteran of a thousand tours of his property and house, Mr. Johnson listens attentively to comments as he opens doors, shoulders movable picture walls, points out the landmark trees, notes influences. Still holding a pencil from an afternoon of drawing, he pointed out the newly renovated bathroom in the brick house, surfaced in marble with dramatic veining. The sculpture gallery has stairs that step in a square spiral down several levels, as at the Guggenheim Museum. "That was a period in the 1970's of unfaithfulness to the Glass House," he remarked.

But all views and paths lead back to the Glass House, which remains the command station for the property. Unlike the other buildings, it shows no sign of age and little sign of fashion.

"I feel it was one of the most significant houses of the period," said Frank Sanchis, a vice president of the National Trust. "It changed the way a house looked, with an open plan and a new relationship between the outside and inside."

"I'd never do it again—I'm numb when I think about the Glass House," Mr. Johnson said. "I feel now it's a vacuum. I never think of the house except for repairs; the most interesting house is the one I'm going to do next."

Still, he defends the house. "I was brought up on a sleeping porch, so I'm used to this," he said. "It's very livable because, like anything else, you adapt to it. When it's too hot you eat or sleep outside. In a house like this, you live in the weather—it's a changing shoal."

As the day draws to a close he walks among the reflections in the glass, through the shadows of trees that fall through the glass, and it is clear that he is completely at home here: the Mies chairs are for him like old familiar armchairs; the Glass House like a comfortable den, and the landscape simply the outermost boundary of his house. From outside, through the glass wall, his figure can be seen as he reclines on the chaise, reading, profiled against the far woods and the sky that, because of the house, have become his second nature.

Robert Dell Vuyosevich

From Reflections No. 8: *The Journal of the School of Architecture*

Semper and Two American Glass Houses

With the appearance of the Farnsworth House and the Glass House in the years just after World War II, a number of articles surfaced offering comparative criticism. Given the formal and programmatic similarities of the houses, and the mentorship provided by Mies van der Rohe for the younger Philip Johnson, the comparison was a natural and obvious one.

Criticism has focused on the compositional differences between the two houses as well as the differences in the architects and buildings which, however indirectly, have influenced them. Philip Johnson, in his book on Mies van der Rohe, traces Mies's ancestry to Schinkel (Neoclassicism), Frank Lloyd Wright (spatial continuity), and the de Stjil movement (overlapping planes in space).[1] Johnson admits to the influences at work in his Glass House: the Acropolis, Ledoux, paintings by Theo van Doesburg, Mondrian, and Malevich, as well as the architecture of Schinkel and Mies van der Rohe.[2] Schinkel appears as the common thread in the work of the two architects.

It is to Gottfried Semper, the greatest German architect of the generation after Schinkel, that this inquiry will look. Whether or not the direct or indirect influence of Semper's writings can be proven, a reading of Semper helps to establish a theoretical framework within which the Farnsworth House of Mies and the Glass House of Johnson can be re-evaluated. Two topics from Semper's writings on architecture and the applied arts are particularly helpful: the two forms of dwelling and the four elements of primitive building, as outlined in Semper's introduction to

Comparative Building Theory (Vergleichende Baulehre, 1850: ms 58, fols. 15-30), as translated by Wolfgang Herrmann.[3] In the opening paragraphs, Semper offers a justification for considering the dwelling as the original type in man's building activity. In an earlier Dresden lecture he had spoken of "the indisputable fact that if not architecture then certainly building, that is, joining materials into an organized form, was first applied to dwellings in the widest sense of the word."[4] To this day, the house, or dwelling, remains the foremost type in which the architect marshals his thought and compositional talents. This is certainly true of Mies and Johnson. Ideas concerning the "joining of materials into an organized form" are manifest in these landmark houses.

The Two Forms of Dwelling. Semper wrote, "We can thus distinguish between two basically different ways in which human dwellings arose. First, the courtyard with its surrounding walls and, within, some open sheds of minor importance, and second, the hut, the freestanding house in its narrowest sense. In the first arrangement, the enclosure, which later became the wall, dominated all other elements of the building, whereas in the second, the roof was the predominant element."[5] Mies's work investigates both types. The brick and concrete houses of 1923 and 1925, their outstretching walls enclosing and directing space, and the court house projects of the 1930s, wherein the space of the court is more conventionally bound, are examples of Mies's preoccupation with court dwelling. In these schemes, as Semper claims, the wall dominates; floor and ceiling, serving to extend space horizontally, are neutral surfaces that accentuate the active role played by the vertical wall in defining and directing space.

Mies's work in the United States demonstrates the development of the second type, the so-called "freestanding hut," evidenced by Mies's first house in America, a guest house/dining pavilion for the Resor family in Jackson Hole, Wyoming, 1937–38, and achieving its fullest expression in the Farnsworth House in Plano, Illinois, 1945–50. One can only speculate that Mies's move to America prompted the switch from court to hut dwelling; the figural space of the European atrium house and piazza is exchanged for the figural solid of the American house in the landscape.

The court and hut in Mies's work, identified as the "court vs. loggia" opposition in Kenneth Frampton's essay "The Glass House Revisited," emerges in the design of the Glass House in New Canaan, Connecticut. Frampton writes: "In deriving his Glass House parti Johnson was caught between a loggia belvedere concept . . . and Mies's prototypical court house. . . . Johnson's early sketches for the Glass House seem to be compounded in part out of Mies's Resor House for Jackson Hole, Wyoming, and in part out of the

Miesian court house—whose introverted form was patently unsuited to the site. . . . In Scheme IV the architect tries to return to the court concept more directly, only to abandon this strategy in Scheme X-A when the project begins to approximate its final form of a glass prism poised on a bluff, looking one way toward the view and the other toward the forespace.[6]

The object/hut, wherein, as Semper says, the roof is the predominant element, surfaces as the chosen type in New Canaan as well as in Plano. In both cases, the inwardly focused court scheme, most appropriate to an urban situation (note Johnson's own Ash Street House, Cambridge, Massachusetts, 1947, or Mies's Lemcke House in Berlin, 1932), has been supplanted by an outwardly focused glass house, Semper's freestanding hut.

The Four Elements of Primitive Building. Having identified the hut as the dwelling type chosen by Mies and Johnson, it is instructive to consult Semper and the four elements of building that constitute the primitive hut. These basic elements are enumerated in *Vergleichende Baulehre* of 1850 and again in his 1851 essay "Die Vier Elemente der Baukunst." At the end of his preface to *Vergleichende Baulehre*, Semper illustrates the four elements with an Indian hut from Trinidad. As Wolfgang Herrmann points out, this appears to be the same Caribbean hut shown at the Great Exhibition of 1851 in London, and referred to in a later lecture as "an instructive illustration

of the system based on the four constructive elements of architecture."[7] This Caribbean hut appears as an illustration in Semper's *Der Stil*, 1860–63, marking the presence of "all the elements of ancient architecture in their most original and unadulterated form: the hearth as centre, the mound surrounded by a framework of poles as terrace, the roof carried by columns, and mats as space enclosure or wall."[8] Hearth, platform, roof, and enclosure constitute the four basic elements of primitive building in Semper's schema.

In *Vergleichende Baulehre*, Semper begins with the hearth: "Before men thought of erecting tents, fences, or huts, they gathered around the open flame, which kept them warm and dry and where they prepared their simple meals. The hearth is the germ, the embryo, of all social institutions.[9] In protecting the hearth, the remaining three elements, the platform, the roof, and enclosure, arise. "Protection of the hearth: There is no need to prove in detail that the protection of the hearth against the rigors of the weather as well as against attacks by wild animals and hostile men was the primary reason for setting apart some space from the surrounding world. . . . Thus, four elements of primitive building arose out of the most immediate needs: the roof, the mound, the enclosure, and, as spiritual center of the whole, the social hearth."[10] Looking at the Farnsworth House and the Glass House in light of these remarks, one finds some notable differences in the articulation and organization of the four elements.

Semper says further, "The hearth has kept its age-old significance up to the present. In every room the center of family life today is still the fireplace.[11] The hearth is more clearly stated as a center in the Glass House. Its placement within a cylinder, which also contains the bathroom, sets it apart from the rectilinear space and the rectilinear objects within that space. The enormous square firebox faces the seating area occupying the central bay of the house. In the Farnsworth House, the firebox is contained within a long wall of Primavera wood panels, two of which serve as doors to bathrooms. A central area for the water pump and heater, as well as the kitchen on the side opposite the fireplace, are additional items contained within the monolithic core. Although the hearth sits near the geometric center of the house and fronts the main seating area, its role as singular center is diffused by the other elements competing for location within the core. With the bedroom wardrobe, a rectangular block finished in teak, Mies complicates the issue by placing a similar solid within the open space. One should note that in the Glass House, the form (rectangular) and the material (teak) of the wardrobe is distinct from that of the brick cylinder, which heightens the role of the latter as center.

Semper continues, ". . . making the settlements secure against the vehemence of the elements was more difficult. Mounds had to be built to protect the hearth against inundation by the nearby river."[12] Though in Johnson's case, protection from flooding is not a consideration (an artificial lake rests almost fifty feet down the hill from the house), the excerpt from Semper is particularly applicable to the Farnsworth House, located in the floodplain of the Fox River. Here, the two floor planes, one forming the entrance terrace at an elevation of +2'-8"+-, the other forming the floor of the house proper and its entrance porch at an elevation of +5'-4"+-, hover above the ground, attached by spot welding to H-columns which rise out of the earth below. The contents of the house are thus protected from flooding by the upper platform which is treated as an independent element in the construction.

It is not without intent that Semper uses the word "mound," so associated with the earth were the early attempts to reshape the ground. The words "platform" and "terrace" are similarly associated with the ground ("terrace" from terra, or earth; "platform," basically the form of plat or ground). Though the ground plane is recreated at Farnsworth as a support for the hearth, it is the nature of its displacement (a floating plane with the actual ground continuing underneath) and its material transformation (a steel-channel frame, sandblasted, spray-painted white and surfaced with travertine) which brings about the sharp distinction between the platform and its progenitor, the earth.

Johnson, while placing the floor three

steps above the ground, associates his platform with the earth. A concrete slab is surfaced in a herringbone pattern of brick and, at the edge, the brick turns down the outside face of a supporting grade beam where it meets the ground. The brick base sits firmly upon the ground, its terra-cotta color accentuating its tie to the earth. Johnson's platform, more closely than that of Mies, approximates the terrace described by Semper in an Assyrian-Chaldean example of primitive building: "The need for these terraces and waterworks must have arisen very early, in fact at a time when the dwelling still consisted of a simple tent. Work on these walls taught the art of masonry, which gradually spread to house building; in its upper parts, the house probably never lost the character of a light construction on a solid substructure. The country lacked timber and in parts even ashlar, whereas the firm clay soil, as soon as it was broken up, offered material ready for use in building. . . . Although kiln-dried bricks were known and used from early times, unburnt sun-dried bricks remained the most commonly used building material."[13] Johnson's choice of brick, effecting a virtual terrace as a solid substructure for the lighter construction above, accords with Semper.

Observations can be made at this point regarding the relationship of elements to one another. In the Farnsworth House, the Primavera wood-surfaced core containing the fireplace is materially distinct from the travertine floor; it is one of a number of elements, including the teak wardrobe, which vie for location within the single space. At the Glass House, Johnson firmly associates hearth and terrace, both made of brick. They are "of the earth" while the steel frame and glass walls which partly contain the cylinder are "other than the earth." Johnson comments on this distinction: "The cylinder, made of the same brick as the platform from which it springs, forming the main motif of the house, was not derived from Mies, but rather from a burnt-out wooden village I saw once where nothing was left but the foundations and chimneys of brick. Over the chimney I slipped a steel cage with a glass skin. The chimney forms the anchor."[14] In the Farnsworth House, no such synthesis of Mother Earth and modernity is attempted, no history or combination of things past and present is imparted to the object; lifted off the ground, the Farnsworth House is positioned as the unqualified symbol of the modern age.

Semper writes, "In regions with a mild climate and in the plain, where people could live in the open air for most of the time, a light tentlike cover against the weather was needed."[15] In this passage citing a tent, and in other descriptions of primitive building, Semper treats the roof and its supports as a single element, given their shared role of providing shelter overhead. This point is critical in Semper's system, and makes it possible to assign the wall a nonsupportive role, that of making enclosure.

Johnson's "steel cage," the roof and its eight H-column supports, is a set of elements distinct from the brick platform and hearth. Both columns and perimeter beams (steel channels) are painted black, and except at the corners where the steel stanchions touch the ground, the cage sits firmly on the brick base. At the Farnsworth House, the details of roof and platform are virtually identical, thus minimizing the distinction between floor and roof. Both are platforms in space, serving to define the "universal space" sandwiched between them.

A further observation can be made regarding the roof. It has been noted that Semper considered the roof and its supports as an element, and in the particular model he chose to illustrate this system, the Indian hut in Trinidad, the wood members comprising the roof and its supports, and the twine that binds them are exposed. "Here is the roof supported by columns of bamboo; its structural parts are tied together with ropes of coconut fiber; it is covered with palm leaves. . . ."[16] From the outside, the "sheathing" of the roof with leaves obscures the connection of roof and support, but from within the hut one sees how the vertical bamboo poles are positioned to relieve the load of a horizontal bamboo pole that picks up the weight of the rafter poles. The tying together of poles at their intersections reveals how the frame works, basketlike, as a unit.

At Farnsworth, the steel joists and their joining with the perimeter channel beam are obscured by a continuous hung ceiling; at the Glass House, a similar white ceiling dominates. From within these two houses, the underside of the roof appears to be an element separate from the supporting structure; the reveal between hung ceiling and perimeter beam heightens this separation. Colin Rowe has commented on the importance of an "uninterrupted horizontal surface" at the ceiling in furthering the spatial objectives of International style buildings."[17] Mies and Johnson pay homage to the International style; both suppress the articulation of the frame and the way it works, in favor of expressing the "universal space" between floor and ceiling.

Semper writes, "But enemies too had to be kept away from the hearth; the much-coveted fields in the plain attracted the envy and rapacity of man, while the herds were exposed to attacks by wild animals. Enclosures, fences, and walls were needed to protect the hearth, and mounds were needed to make it safe from flooding and also to espy the enemy from afar."[18] At the Farnsworth House and the Glass House, the making of secure walls to protect one from one's enemies is hardly an issue; both structures open up to the surrounding landscape, a secure and private place. A curtain wall of plate glass encased in thin steel mullions provides both houses with the desired enclosure and transparency of surface; the treatment of the wall and its relationship to the other elements varies significantly.

Mies concerns himself with differentiating the roof and its supports (his structure) from the enclosing skin. The curtain wall at Farnsworth runs just behind the columns, and the reveal between the mullions and the H-columns or channel beams makes clear the separation of support and non-supporting enclosure. In the Glass House, as Frampton has argued most clearly, the structure is "suppressed"; the steel columns are set inside the glass wall, except at the corners, where the column is seen to support the perimeter beam.[19] The curtain wall, its thin mullions set out beyond the plane of the steel frame, asserts itself as an independent element bounding the volume of space within. The greater reflectivity of the glass at the Glass House further accentuates the surface quality of the curtain wall. The wall predominates in Johnson's work; in Mies's it is reduced to "*beinahe nichts*, 'almost nothing'" and structure is preeminent.[20]

Semper's remarks on Assyrian-Chaldean architecture challenge our understanding of the wall: "The primary material establishing the norm for the vertical enclosure was not the stone wall but a material that, though less durable, for a long time influenced the development of architecture as strongly as stone, metal, and timber. I mean the hurdle, the mat, and the carpet. . . . Using wickerwork for setting apart one's property and for floor mats for protection against heat and cold far preceded making even the roughest masonry. Wickerwork was the original motif

of the wall. . . . Hanging carpets remained the true walls; they were the visible boundaries of a room. The often solid walls behind them were necessary for reasons that had nothing to do with the creation of space; they were needed for protection, for supporting a load, for their permanence, etc. Wherever the need for these secondary functions did not arise, carpets remained the only means for separating space. Even where solid walls became necessary, they were only the invisible structure hidden behind the true representatives of the wall, the colorful carpets that the walls served to hold and support. It was therefore the covering of the wall that was primarily and essentially of spatial and architectural significance; the wall itself was secondary."[21] This passage opens a floodgate of possibilities in further interpreting the two houses.

One thinks of Mies's earlier work (Barcelona, Tugendhat) in advancing the free plan in modern architecture, wherein the supporting columns are differentiated from the walls which merely enclose or direct space. The sensuous materials employed (green Tinian marble, vert antique marble, a tawny onyx, clear, gray, and bottle-green glass, a red silk drape at Barcelona; tawny-gold onyx, black and pale brown Macassar ebony, silver-gray Shantung silk curtains at Tugendhat)[22] evoke the richness of the earlier hung carpets described by Semper. Enclosure was simply made by hanging velvet and silk at the Exposition de la Mode in Berlin, 1927: "Mies and Frau Lilly Reich defined spaces within the large exhibition hall by draping lengths of black, red, and orange velvet and gold, silver, black, and lemon-yellow silk fabric over straight and curved rods which were suspended from the ceiling."[23] The silk curtain makes repeat performances in both the Farnsworth House and the Glass House, providing privacy, when desired, and helping to control the extremes of heat and cold.

But it is the glass curtain wall (the retention of the word "curtain" in the phrase, thus preserving the essential "motif" of the wall, would amuse Semper) which constitutes the true skin and enclosure at the Glass House and at Farnsworth. The skin holds in the space, given its counter-tendency to spread out horizontally between roof and platform. This is evidenced even more so in the Glass House, where there is the greater "presence" of that surface. And it is in the greater reflectivity of that glass surface that the enclosing wall alludes most subtly to its primitive forebear. The surrounding foliage is reflected in the glass wall; patterns of leaves and branches animate the surface, recalling the ancient carpets.

Semper discusses the wall, its material transformation without the consequent loss of the essential motif: "The covering of the wall retained this meaning even when other materials than carpets were used. . . . For a long time the character of the new covering followed that of the prototype. The artists who created the painted

or sculpted decoration on wood, stucco, stone, or metal, following a tradition that they were hardly conscious of, imitated the colorful embroideries of the age-old carpet-walls."[24] Though Semper acknowledged the transformation of motifs over time and could imagine a thousandfold variations upon the four elements of construction in their treatment and combination, it is doubtful that the possibilities inherent in reflective glass for yet another transposition of the age-old motif ever occurred to him.

And certainly the use of steel in these two twentieth-century houses would give him pause. While Semper spoke well of the technical triumph of the Crystal Palace, he discouraged the use of iron in architecture, in a passage reminiscent of Ruskin: "So much is certain that . . . architecture . . . must not have anything to do with this quasi-invisible material when it is a question of mass effects. . . ."[25] We hear this architect of a century ago passing judgment on Mies and Johnson when he calls the Jardins d'Hiver of 1847 an "enormous glass box (which) absorbs everything" and "leaves too small a share to architecture."[26]

These two glass houses can hardly be criticized for leaving "too small a share to architecture." There is a thoughtfulness and rigor in their assemblage which belies their simple nature. Semper helps us to forge relationships between these houses and those of their progenitors, to recognize archetypal elements which have preoccupied people through the ages. These two houses demonstrate a transformative process that connects, and at the same time separates, objects across time and place. We recognize the modernity of these structures; at the same time, we are witness to the "freestanding hut" in its original and simple state.

Notes

1. Philip Johnson, *Mies van der Rohe* (New York: Museum of Modern Art), 1978, pp. 9–30.
2. Kenneth Frampton, "The Glass House Revisited," in *Philip Johnson: Processes.* Catalogue 9 (New York: Institute for Architecture and Urban Studies, 1978), p. 39.
3. Wolfgang Herrmann, *Gottfried Semper: In Search of Architecture* (Cambridge, Mass.: MIT Press, 1984).
4. Gottfried Semper, in Herrmann, p. 168.
5. Semper, fols, 23-24, in Herrmann, p. 201.
6. Frampton, p. 42.
7. Herrmann, p. 169.
8. Semper, *Der Stil*, in Herrmann, p. 169.
9. Semper, fols. 18-20, in Herrmann, p. 198.
10. Semper, fols. 21-22, in Herrmann, p. 199.
11. Semper, fols. 18-20, in Herrmann, p. 198.
12. Semper, fols. 21-22, in Herrmann, p. 199.
13. Semper, fols. 104-106, in Herrmann, p. 211.
14. Johnson, in Frampton, p. 51.
15. Semper, fols. 21-22, in Herrmann, p. 199.
16. Semper, in Herrmann, p. 169.
17. Colin Rowe, "Neo-'Classicism' and Modern Architecture II" in *The Mathematics of the Ideal Villa and Other Essays* (Cambridge, Mass.: MIT Press, 1984), p. 143.
18. Semper, fols. 21-22, in Herrmann, p. 199.
19. Frampton, p. 51.
20. Johnson, p. 140.
21. Semper, fols. 94-98, in Herrmann, pp. 204–206.
22. David Spaeth, *Mies van der Rohe* (New York: Rizzoli, 1985), pp. 75–76.
23. Spaeth, p. 52.
24. Semper, fols. 98-100, in Herrmann, p. 206.
25. Semper, in Herrmann, p. 175.
26. Ibid., p. 176.

Acknowledgments

Grateful acknowledgment is made to the following for permission to reprint the following previously published material:

Architectural Digest: "Architecture: Philip Johnson—The Glass House Revisited" by Vincent Scully. Courtesy *Architectural Digest* © 1986. All rights reserved.

Architectural Record: "Architect's Retreat" by Walter Wagner from *Architectural Record*, July 1983 issue. Copyright 1983 by McGraw-Hill Inc. All rights reserved. Reprinted by permission of the publisher.

Rosamond Bernier: "Improving His View" by Rosamond Bernier from *House & Garden*, June 1986. Reprinted by permission of the author.

Columbia University, School of Architecture: "The Glass House Revisited" by Kenneth Frampton from *Catalogue 9*, Sept./Oct. 1978. Reprinted by permission.

Peter Eisenman and Philip Johnson: "Introduction" by Peter Eisenman and "Full Scale False Scale" by Philip Johnson from *Philip Johnson Writings* edited by Peter Eisenman, Oxford University Press, 1978. Reprinted by permission of the authors.

Joel Goldblatt, Executor of the Estate of Arthur Drexler: "Architecture Opaque and Transparent" by Arthur Drexler from *Interiors & Industrial Design*, October 1949. Reprinted by permission.

Philip Johnson: "House in New Canaan, Connecticut" by Philip Johnson from *Architectural Review*, September 1950. Reprinted by permission of the author.

Lotus: "The House of Dreams and Memories" by Francesco Dal Co from *Lotus 35*, 1982. Reprinted by permission of *Lotus*, Milan.

The New York Times: "Johnson and His Glass House: Reflections" by Joseph Giovannini from *The New York Times*, July 16, 1987. Copyright © 1987 by The New York Times Company. Reprinted by permission.

The New Yorker: Excerpts from "Profiles: Forms Under Light" by Calvin Tomkins from *The New Yorker*, May 23, 1977. Copyright © 1977 by Calvin Tomkins. Reprinted by permission. All rights reserved.

Oxford University Press: Extract from *Philip Johnson Writings* by Peter Eisenman. Copyright © 1979 by Oxford University Press, Inc. Reprinted by permission.

Perspecta: The Yale Architectural Journal: "Johnson" by Philip Johnson, originally published in *Perspecta 7: The Yale Architectural Journal*, pp. 3–8, 1961 and "Whence and Whither: The Processional Element in Architecture" by Philip Johnson originally published in *Perspecta 9/10: The Yale Architectural Journal*. Reprinted by permission.

Acknowledgments

Reflections: "Semper and Two American Glass Houses" by Robert Dell Vuyosevich from *Reflections No. 8: The Journal of the School of Architecture*. Reprinted by permission.

Robert A.M. Stern Architects: "The Evolution of Philip Johnson's Glass House, 1947–1948 by Robert A.M. Stern from *Oppositions*, Fall 1977. Reprinted by permission.

Time Inc.: "The Duke of Xanadu at Home" by Robert Hughes from *Time*, October 26, 1970. Copyright © 1970 by Time Inc. Reprinted by permission.

Illustration Credits

Pages

33 Photograph of the Glass House by Alexandre Georges.

34 Photograph of the Brick Guest House and the Glass House. Courtesy of Philip Johnson.

35 Photograph of the Glass House. Courtesy of Philip Johnson.

36 Photograph of the Glass House and the Sculpture Gallery by Richard Payne.

37 Photograph of interior of the Glass House by Ezra Stoller.

38 Photograph of interior of the Glass House. Courtesy of Philip Johnson.

39 Photograph of interior of the Glass House by Norman McGrath.

40 Photograph of the Glass House by Ezra Stoller.

41 Photographs of the Guest House, interior of the Guest House, and interior of the Glass House. All courtesy of Philip Johnson.

42 Site plan of the Glass House. Courtesy of Philip Johnson.

43 Site plan of the Glass House. Courtesy of Philip Johnson. Plan of the Glass House. Courtesy of Philip Johnson.

53 Photograph of the Glass House by Ezra Stoller.

70–71 Map of the Glass House Compound by Dennis O'Brien.

125 Photograph of the Glass House and the Guest House by Ezra Stoller.

126 Photograph of the interior of the Guest House by Alexandre Georges.

127 Plans of the Guest House. All courtesy of Philip Johnson.

128 Photograph of the Pavilion by Ezra Stoller.

129 Plan of the Pavilion. Courtesy of Philip Johnson.

130 Photograph of the Painting Gallery by Ezra Stoller.

131 Photograph of interior of the Painting Gallery by Norman McGrath.

132 Photograph of interior of the Painting Gallery by Norman McGrath.

133 Photograph of interior of the Painting Gallery by Norman McGrath.

134 Site plan of the Painting Gallery. Courtesy of Philip Johnson. Plan of the Painting Gallery. Courtesy of Philip Johnson.

135 Photograph of the Sculpture Gallery by Norman McGrath.

136–37 Photograph of interior of the Sculpture Gallery by Norman McGrath.

138 Photograph of the Sculpture Gallery by Norman McGrath.

139 Plan of the Sculpture Gallery. Courtesy of Philip Johnson.

140 Photograph of the Study by Richard Payne.

141 Photograph of interior of the Study by Richard Payne.

142 Plans of the Study. All courtesy of Philip Johnson.

143 Photograph of the entrance gate by Richard Bryant.

144 Photograph of the Lincoln Kirstein Tower by Norman McGrath.

145 Photograph of the Ghost House by Norman McGrath.

157 Photograph of the Glass House by Norman McGrath.

About the Editors

David Whitney is a freelance exhibition curator and editor. He lives in New York City.

Jeffrey Kipnis is Associate Professor of Theory and Design at Ohio State University's School of Architecture. He is a frequent contributor to journals and anthologies of architectural criticism.